THE PIRATE

Plays by S. N. Behrman

THE SECOND MAN

METEOR

SERENA BLANDISH

BRIEF MOMENT

BIOGRAPHY

RAIN FROM HEAVEN

END OF SUMMER

AMPHITRYON 38
  *Adapted from the
  French of Jean Giraudoux*

WINE OF CHOICE

NO TIME FOR COMEDY

THE TALLEY METHOD

THE PIRATE

S. N. BEHRMAN

THE
PIRATE

RANDOM HOUSE · NEW YORK

Copyright, 1943, by

S. N. BEHRMAN

First Printing

The Pirate was suggested by an idea
in a play by Ludwig Fulda

MANUFACTURED IN THE UNITED STATES OF AMERICA

For

RUDOLF K. KOMMER
fr. Cz.

IN MEMORIAM: LUDWIG FULDA

ALL through the preliminary tour of this play I kept hearing, from people who had met him, about Ludwig Fulda. He had lectured in America in 1906 and again in 1913 and covered, evidently, the same ground which his play was to traverse, after his death, thirty years later. In Indianapolis and in Cincinnati retired music critics and editors told me about the impression Fulda had made on them: suave, cultured, personable. On these two trips he lectured in more than thirty cities and sixteen universities. He wrote a book about us, *American Impressions,* which was so enthusiastic about this country that he was criticized for it in Germany.

His most famous play in Germany was a drama in verse called *Der Talisman.* This is based on an old fairy tale of an ingenious tailor who persuades the Emperor that he is selling him a stately garment which has the property of visibility only to the wise and to the loyal. Actually this raiment is very ordinary underwear. Since he is surrounded by yes-men and sycophants the entire court goes into raptures about the wonder and the beauty of this garment. It is a child who comes out with the truth: "But the Emperor is naked!" A courtier, attempting to comfort the embarrassed monarch, utters two lines which reverberated shudderingly throughout Germany:

IN MEMORIAM: LUDWIG FULDA

"Ihr musst, mein Herr, darob euch nicht erbosen
Ihr bleibt ein Koenig auch in Unterhosen."

Roughly translated they are:

"Sire, you need not be annoyed
You remain a King even in your underwear."

This was as great a sensation as the use of the word
"bloody" in Shaw's *Pygmalion!* It infringed upon the notion
of an emperor's divinity and the Kaiser was distressed and
vengeful. When the Schiller Prize was awarded to the poet
the Emperor refused his sanction and the prize was with-
drawn. Nevertheless, in 1914, Fulda defended the Kaiser in
magazine articles in this country. With that mystical imper-
meability which Roussy de Sales in his wonderful book points
to as characteristic of even the best Germans, Fulda spoke of
"the ethical seriousness of the German Army!" When the
rash of nationalism had subsided after the First World War,
he devoted his talents to the cause of German democracy.
Essentially, he was a passionate liberal and democrat.

In 1889, with Maximilian Harden and Theodore Wolff,
Fulda organized Die Freie Buhne which had a revolutionary
influence in the German theatre. This group produced Ger-
hart Hauptmann and made his reputation; it started the
literary and theatrical trend known as "naturalism." As a
translator Fulda was inspired. He made enchanting transcrip-
tions into German of Rostand's *Cyrano de Bergerac* and of
the plays of Molière. *Robinson Island,* a play of his published
in 1895, anticipated the main idea of J. M. Barrie's *The Admirable Crichton.*

viii

IN MEMORIAM: LUDWIG FULDA

My friend Bruno Frank tells me that he last saw Fulda in Switzerland just after the advent of Hitler. It was impossible for him to assimilate the concept of no longer being considered a German. He was completely bewildered by what had happened both to Germany and to him. He was over seventy. He had held high honors in his native country. He was distinguished in philanthropy and in letters and yet here he was in Switzerland, with his country making a virtue and a slogan of the racial principle that had ousted him. Ultimately he returned to Germany, where the production of his plays was forbidden. When he died in Berlin in 1939, no German paper was permitted to publish an obituary.

And yet a conceit of his, freely adapted, has survived the horrors of these two decades, and here it is played by two of the foremost artists in the American theatre. One day, a half century ago, Fulda must have been seized with a comic idea: a world-famous pirate with an itch for respectability retires to a small community, marries and becomes the village censor. It must have seemed pretty good to Fulda and he sat down and wrote his play, *Die Seerauber*. Is it not a comment on the absurdity of the effort to erect, against freedom of any thought whatever, the tallest dike in history, that it should be so porous that even a little comic idea like this can seep through and flourish bountifully in another land, in another language, in another cultural and intellectual climate altogether? Despite the grimaces of the *Herrenvolk* and the obscenities of the Gestapo, Fulda's smile at hypocritical pomposity has survived. Surely, if this small laughter can evade the vast censorships and the horrendous propagandas, what chance have these new overlords, with their cosmic structures lasting a thousand years, to shut out major ideas and more inspired indignations? The Emperor is in his underwear indeed!

It is agreeable to be able to make to Ludwig Fulda some sort of return in kind. In the freemasonry of art, he was evidently a moving spirit—toward the internationalism beyond Geneva to which in a thousand years we may attain.

S. N. BEHRMAN.

The Pirate was first produced by The Playwrights' Company and The Theatre Guild on November 23, 1942, at the Martin Beck Theatre, New York City, with the following cast:

MANUELA	Lynn Fontanne
PEDRO VARGAS	Alan Reed
ISABELLA	Lea Penman
MANGO SELLER	Juanita Hall
FISHERBOY	Albert Popwell
INES	Estelle Winwood
CAPUCHO	James O'Neill
LIZARDA	Muriel Rahn
ESTABAN	Robert Emhardt
DON BOLO	Walter Mosby
TRILLO	Maurice Ellis
SERAFIN	Alfred Lunt
VICEROY	Clarence Derwent
SEMPER	David Bethea
HERMIT	William Le Massena
MAIDS TO MANUELA	Ruby Greene Anna Jackson Louvinia White
MAID TO ISABELLA	Inez Matthews
VICEROY'S GUARDS	Guy Monypenny Peter Garey

MEMBERS OF SERAFIN'S TROUPE, SOLDIERS AND TOWNS-
PEOPLE:
David Bethea, Bruce Howard, Martha Jones, Jules
Johnson, Clare Keith, Fredye Marshall, Charles
Swain, Eloise Uggams, Joseph Washington, Carol
Wilson, Jeffrey Etheridge.

MUSICIANS:
Emilio Denti, Emmet Matthews, John Dixon,
Adolphus Cheatham, Wilbur De Paris, Eddie Gibbs,
John Brown, Max Rich, Herbert Cowens.

Staged by ALFRED LUNT *and* JOHN C. WILSON
Music by HERBERT KINGSLEY
Settings by LEMUEL AYERS
Costumes by MILES WHITE
Dances by FELICIA SOREL

SCENES

ACT ONE

SCENE I—The Patio of Pedro Vargas' House.
SCENE II—A mountain road.
SCENE III—The public square.

ACT TWO

Manuela's bedroom. Same day.

ACT THREE

The public square. That evening.

The action takes place in a small village in the West Indies early in the nineteenth century.

ACT ONE

ACT ONE

Scene I

Scene: *A small village in Santo Domingo; early in the nineteenth century. It is the middle of a very hot afternoon in midsummer.*

At Rise: PEDRO's *patio.* PEDRO *garrulously asleep in the hammock. A rabbit's foot is tied around his neck and on the pillow beside him are a four-leaf clover and a good-luck penny, both of which* PEDRO *has picked up.*

MANUELA, *her back to the audience, sits beside him, fanning him with a large palmetto fan. She is deeply absorbed in a black-covered book which she holds in her other hand. It appears to be a Bible. Three or four colored girls, close together, looking in their bright dresses like a display of rare tropical fruits in an open-air market, crouch at the edge of the patio, singing softly, a composition sounding if possible sensuously liturgical. To the rhythm of this singing,* MANUELA *fans, and to the rhythm of the singing also, though he is probably not aware of it,* PEDRO, *her husband, snores.*

PEDRO
(Bursting out in his sleep)
Sixty! I won't pay a peso over sixty! (MANUELA *rises, crosses*

3

to the girls, raising her fan to stop their singing for a moment.
Out of his haggling sleep) Not sixty-two—not sixty-one—
sixty . . .

MANUELA

Please pay it, dear! Sleep, beloved! Sleep! (*Waves girls off*
with fan. They exit, singing softly.)

PEDRO
(*Like a catapult*)

Sixty!

MANUELA
(*To reassure him*)
He'll sell, husband. They always do.

PEDRO

Not a farthing over—sixty.

MANUELA
(*Comes back to her chair and starts to read again, fanning*
PEDRO *meanwhile*)
My parents did. And at your figure. And what a figure!

PEDRO

Robber! Cheat! (*He turns over on his side, the veiling over*
his face that protects him from the flies falls to the ground.
She picks it up, covers his face with it—shoos away a hum-
ming fly that wants to settle on his nose.)

4

MANUELA

Sleep, my darling. Sleep, beloved. Sleep, my gallant trader! (*Her voice tinkles with friendly irony.*)

PEDRO

(*In triumph*)

Sold!

MANUELA

There, now, you may rest easy. (PEDRO *snores orchestrally—* MANUELA *pensively*) Sleep, beloved, sleep. (*The snore subsides.* MANUELA *reads her Bible. She becomes so caught that she forgets to fan.* ISABELLA GALVEZ, *the Widow Galvez, enters the patio. She is plump and amiable.*)

ISABELLA

What a touching domestic scene!

MANUELA

Isabella—shh . . .

ISABELLA

The devoted wife—reads her camouflaged Bible—fans her sleeping spouse!

MANUELA

Isabella, don't wake him.

ISABELLA

What's he got there—around his neck?

5

MANUELA

It's his rabbit's foot, and a four-leaf clover, and a lucky penny. He's very superstitious. Didn't you know that? He always sleeps that way—festooned with amulets.

PEDRO

(*Stirring*)

I won't pay it—never!

MANUELA

That's right, darling, don't pay it! (*To* ISABELLA) He feels better when he doesn't pay it. Even in his sleep he barters. He keeps adding and subtracting. . . .

ISABELLA

Adding, mostly. No wonder he's the richest man in town.

MANGO WOMAN

(*Her head pops in suddenly at the window over* PEDRO's *head.*)

Mangoes!

MANUELA

Shh—no—no—go away. (*As* MANGO WOMAN *disappears,* PEDRO *rolls over, noisily sterterous.* MANUELA *crosses to hammock and covers* PEDRO *with netting.*)

ISABELLA

But, Manuela, tell me—where is he?

6

MANUELA
(Pretends not to know)

Who?

ISABELLA

Estramudo, of course.

MANUELA

Oh, the book . . .

ISABELLA

Certainly. How sly you are—covering it up like a Bible!

MANUELA

Well, you know how strict Pedro is. But, oh, Isabella, I can't thank you enough for giving me this novel. Estramudo, how wonderful he is, how agile! He's just escaped!

ISABELLA

From the harem?

MANUELA

No, no—from the French privateers.

ISABELLA
(Takes book from MANUELA*)*

Oh, wait! Wait till he gets to the harem! (*She giggles lasciviously.*)

MANUELA
(Sits)

Do such men live? Do they breathe the air? Do they ride the waves?

ISABELLA

Estramudo does. He's been captured and killed and drowned. He's suffered every variety of death. But he always pops up. He's escaped in a thousand disguises. But they'll never get him.

MANUELA

Oh, no.

ISABELLA

(*With naive boastfulness*)

I know just what he looks like. I have a cousin who saw him in a theatre in Seville.

MANUELA

(*Incredulously*)

She saw him!

ISABELLA

She saw him. (PEDRO *snores*. MANUELA *fans him*.)

MANUELA

Sleep, baby, sleep.

ISABELLA

He's in good voice today.

MANUELA

Under the heavy artillery I can read.

ISABELLA

You are too lenient with him. Why don't you rebel?

THE PIRATE

MANUELA

A bargain is a bargain.

ISABELLA

It wasn't your bargain. It was your mother's.

MANUELA

Nevertheless it was made.

ISABELLA

He cheats in all his bargains. Cheat in yours.

MANUELA

Isabella! He supports my father and mother.

ISABELLA

He's supposed to.

MANUELA

He does what he's supposed to, so must I.

ISABELLA

I can't understand it. I'll never understand—that you, the most sensitive of all us girls in the convent—the bookworm, the class poet, in fact, should be married to that pumpkin.

MANUELA

Pumpkin! Why, Isabella! He's traveled all over the world. He sold cannonballs, you know, to all the governments. Now really, Isabella, you cannot call a man like Pedro a pumpkin.

ISABELLA

Well, he's got a frightful temper. All the neighbors hear him screaming at you.

MANUELA

Oh, that doesn't mean anything. Actually he's very sweet to me—very generous. He loves good food. . . .

ISABELLA

Obviously.

MANUELA

And when I plan an especially good meal, he praises me.

ISABELLA

Well, you put a good face on it, Manuela, and that's gallant of you. But—do you remember how we used to plan whom we'd marry—the wonderful romances we used to spin—you, Manuela, you especially. . . .

MANUELA

That was adolescence. . . . You know, Isabella, I think the Gulf Stream did us in!

ISABELLA

Everything around here is blamed on the Gulf Stream.

MANUELA

But it's so. A caprice of the Gulf Stream ruined father's fisheries. Of course he always gambled away half his income, but when his income ceased altogether he went right on gambling. He told me—just when I was considering Pedro— he told me, father did, that if he had to stop gambling he would die. So you see, Isabella, it was a case of life and death. (PEDRO *shifts noisily*.)

PEDRO

Sold!

MANUELA

(*Relieved*)

Oh, I'm so glad, dear. (*To* ISABELLA *as* PEDRO *snores in triumph*) He's concluded the deal. Listen. Victory march.

ISABELLA

I bet it was a bankruptcy sale. . . .

MANUELA

(*As the hammock creaks with* PEDRO'*s weight*)

Oh, dear, I must reinforce the hammock. You know he never sleeps in a bed—always in a hammock. Isn't that curious—always in a hammock?

ISABELLA

That must add to your sense of insecurity.

MANUELA

You wouldn't think a prosaic business man would have so many odd habits.

ISABELLA

You're a martyr.

MANUELA
(*Rising*)

A martyr.

ISABELLA

I don't believe in it.

MANUELA
(*Crossing to hammock to cover* PEDRO *with netting*)
I have luxury—my parents are provided for—and I have my dreams. Please go away, Isabella, before he wakes. You know he disapproves of you.

ISABELLA

Two officers from the Capitol are here tonight. They belong to the viceroy's private guard. They're on leave.

MANUELA

How nice for them!

ISABELLA

First lieutenants. Stunning in their uniforms.

MANUELA

I'm sure they are.

ISABELLA

Join us. Join us tonight. A foursome.

PEDRO

Forty! Ridiculous!

ISABELLA

What do you say, Manuela?

MANUELA

No.

ISABELLA

Why not?

MANUELA

A bargain is a bargain. . . . My real life I prefer to keep scrupulous and tidy. My dream life—impossibly romantic.

ISABELLA

Mix 'em. Mix 'em.

MANUELA

No, Isabella, not for me, but thank you very much. Please, go away before he wakes up. (*It is too late.* PEDRO *sits bolt upright, wide awake.*)

PEDRO

(*As he emerges from his dream*)
Cheaters! Robbers! Where's my rabbit's foot?

MANUELA

Around your neck, darling. (PEDRO *clutches at it, reassured.*)

PEDRO

(*Suddenly seeing* ISABELLA)
What are you doing on my property? I thought I'd forbidden you to talk to her?

ISABELLA

So broad-beamed—so narrow-minded.

PEDRO

She's a loose widow.

MANUELA

(*Pleading for tolerance*)

If she is a widow, is it not God's will? Is survival in itself an act of infidelity?

ISABELLA

My husband, I'll have you know, died happy.

PEDRO

He died ignorant!

MANUELA

I'll do my best not to survive you, Pedro. I'll try!

PEDRO

I won't have this baggage on my premises.

MANUELA

Go away, Isabella.

ISABELLA

And I won't have your insults.

PEDRO

Strumpet!

THE PIRATE

MANUELA
(*Pleading*)

Isabella!

ISABELLA

Look at the beam in your own eye. Your wife may be technically faithful, but mentally, you might as well know it, she takes excursions.

MANUELA
(*Frightened*)

Isabella, please!

ISABELLA

Always at her prayers, eh? Well, look!

PEDRO
(*Reaching for the book*)

Put down the good book. You defile it.

ISABELLA

I defile it, do I? Well, look! (PEDRO *takes book from* ISABELLA, *goes back to hammock and sits reading book.*)

MANUELA
(*Terrified*)

Isabella!

ISABELLA

I'm sorry, my dear, I couldn't take any more from that old skinflint. Good job for you, too. Clear the air. You haven't the courage to rebel by yourself. I'll make you. Maybe after

you've had it out you'll join me tonight after all. You can
have the tall one.

PEDRO

(*Looking up*)

The tall one!

ISABELLA

Six foot one. He's as tall this way (*She makes a gesture
reaching up*) as you are that way. (*Makes a gesture reaching
out. She flounces out.*)

PEDRO

(*Staring at the book. Actually he is frightened*)

What is this? Where did you get this? Where did this
come from?

MANUELA

(*Weakly*)

Pedro, please . . . (*He stares at the page before him.*)

PEDRO

(*Reading from the title page*)

"The Glorious Adventures of Estramudo the Pirate."

MANUELA

Just a silly little novel.

PEDRO

"Together with a full and uncensored account of his travels
far and wide."

MANUELA

Just meant to pass the time.

16

PEDRO

"His intrigues at the courts of Europe . . ."

MANUELA

Of no importance whatever . . .

PEDRO

". . . and among the potentates of Asia, together with . . ."
(*He stops for breath.*)

MANUELA

(*Picks it up from memory*)
"Together with a brave account of his adventures with the
caliphates of the Turks, including his sensational escape, together with nine of the wives, from the Palace of the Grand
Vizier himself! Together with . . ."

PEDRO

Stop it! Stop it! You know it by heart!

MANUELA

Only the title page.

PEDRO

The greatest criminal alive!

MANUELA

He's not a criminal! He only attacks other pirates. And,
Pedro, whenever he lands, he distributes alms. He's the Robin
Hood of the seas!

PEDRO

Romanticizing a criminal—this robber—this murderer—this
—this . . .

MANUELA

This Estramudo—this improbable man—Estramudo.

PEDRO

You linger over his name.

MANUELA

It has a cadence. Of all my heroes—Napoleon . . .

PEDRO

He's rotting in St. Helena where this fellow should be.

MANUELA

Lord Byron . . .

PEDRO

(*Contemptuously*)

Poet!

MANUELA

Of all of them Estramudo's name is the loveliest. Don't
you think so, Pedro—just as mere sound? Or do you prefer
Shelley? No. Too short. Can't get into it. Oh, read this,
Pedro, it'll get you out of yourself.

PEDRO

I don't want to get out of myself!

18

THE PIRATE

MANUELA

I know, but I do wish . . . Oh, Pedro, I don't want to sound priggish, but I do wish you'd change a little to the spiritual side.

PEDRO

(Sits bolt upright in hammock)
The spiritual side! No one is more regular at Mass than I am. Didn't I restore the belfry?

MANUELA

You restored the belfry.

PEDRO

I distribute prayer books among the poor, don't I?

MANUELA

You do, darling, you do.

PEDRO

(Lies flat on his back, contemplating his benefactions)
Well now, how can I be more spiritual than that?

MANUELA

Perhaps spiritual is not the word. Perhaps I should have said imaginative. That's it, I do wish you could be more imaginative.

PEDRO

I don't know what you're talking about.

MANUELA

(*Wistfully*)

For one thing, you're always sleeping. You're out all day on your business deals, and the moment you get home you make straight for your hammock. . . . It's so—non-co-operative.

PEDRO

I work hard! I'm exhausted!

MANUELA

And then, darling, you do neglect your personal appearance.

PEDRO

(*Petulant*)

I can't help that. Everything I eat goes to my stomach. I'm glandular.

MANUELA

You're stodgy.

PEDRO

What do you want me to do?

MANUELA

Ah, Pedro, is life all business, eating and sleeping and philanthropy? I've never been outside this village where I was born. Is there no realm beyond—no horizon beyond our horizon?

PEDRO

No.

20

THE PIRATE

MANUELA

(*Passionately*)

I long for a glimpse of the world beyond this saucer in the hills. I want—I want . . .

PEDRO

Well, what do you want?

MANUELA

I want to be able to love you. I want to invest the gross reality of our marriage with some of the quality of my dreams.

PEDRO

No investments.

MANUELA

Except for profit—I know. Oh, Pedro, I have infinite love to lavish if only you'll try.

PEDRO

I won't have you dreaming. No trips—even mentally! It's sinful.

MANUELA

On the contrary, it's the saving virtue. So far I have not dabbled in reality. I want to center my affections in you—but you make it difficult—so difficult.

PEDRO

(*Rises, advances on her.* MANUELA *backs away from him*)

How dare you criticize me, sentimental numbskull! I support your extravagant mother, don't I? And your gambling father, don't I? While you're mooning over trash like this! (PEDRO *snatches book away from her.*)

MANUELA

Please—it's a unique copy.

PEDRO

That's too many. (*Throws book out of the window*) There —it will feed the fishes. It will corrupt even them. I shan't eat the catch for several Fridays.

MANUELA
(*With tragic resignation*)
It belonged to Isabella. (*Now* MANUELA's *despair is complete. Somehow the novel has become a symbol to her of an imaginative if not of an actual freedom. It is gone. She stands bereft.* CAPUCHO *and* INES, *her father and mother, come in.* INES, *incredibly and flamboyantly dressed, looks like the tails of nine peacocks.* CAPUCHO, *the gambler, is a little, wizened man who smokes a cheroot and has, since his marriage thirty-five years ago, lost the power of speech.* INES *has it and exercises it. She is very sycophantic to* PEDRO *as the source of all the good things of life.* CAPUCHO *fondles, in the side pocket of his gold-braided trousers, a leather cylinder containing his beloved dice. In his mind, he is constantly rolling dice.*)

PEDRO
(*With heavy sarcasm*)
Here are the lady and gentleman now! Well, peacock!

THE PIRATE

INES

(With an effulgent smile)

Peacock, he calls me! How he knows the way to a woman's heart! Pedro, my rising sun. Pedro, my evening star.

PEDRO

None of your palaver. It's no good any more.

INES

(Severely—to MANUELA*)*

Manuela, have you been remiss?

PEDRO

Ah! Even she knows!

INES

(Placidly)

I know this. My Pedro, my benefactor, my new-found son . . .

PEDRO

Stop calling me new-found—I've been here for years.

INES

My life began with the day of your arrival.

PEDRO

On the day of my arrival you had just celebrated your fifty-eighth birthday. (CAPUCHO *rattles his dice*) Stop rattling those infernal dice.

23

INES

Stop rattling, Capucho! He lost today. He lost thirty pesos. He never wins. True, Pedro, my eagle, reckoned by time, you speak truth. But endowed by happiness, gilded by joy, you are new-found—and I am reborn.

PEDRO

Shut up!

INES
(*To* MANUELA)

What have you done, daughter, that your Pedro, whose temper is like drifted butter, whose nature is like the embrace of spring, what have you done that he is curdled? What have you done? (MANUELA *cannot speak. She shakes her head, her eyes filled with tears. She turns away.* INES *turns to her husband, cracks down on him so he jumps*) Capucho! Your brains, the tidbit you have, are in those dice. (*To* PEDRO) That's why they never win—they're not weighted. (*She laughs raucously*) Discipline your daughter! (CAPUCHO *shrugs his shoulders, begins to rattle*) Stop rattling!

PEDRO

He discipline! Fine disciplinarian! I'm sick of it. No more allowance. No more finery. No more gambling. I'm through.

INES

He must have been sorely tried—sorely tried. That nature as beneficent as April rain! Manuela, you are selfish, you have

24

always been selfish. You contaminate the source, you curdle the source. Manuela, my girl, you have a God for a husband, and what do you do? Morning and night you should burn incense, you should offer prayers and thanks. . . .

PEDRO

Enough—enough. I'm sleepy.

INES
(*Quivering with solicitude*)
He's sleepy. You hear? He's sleepy. He wants to rest. Well, do you hear me? Pedro, my lamb, Pedro, my exquisite zebra, let your mother make you comfortable. . . . (*She tries to lead him to the hammock.*)

PEDRO
(*Shaking her off, surly*)
Let me alone, speckled adder. (*He goes to the hammock by himself and lies down.*)

INES
(*To* MANUELA)
Ah, how sorely you must have tried him! How sorely! I will take you in hand, young lady. The birch—you are not yet too old for the birch (*At this point,* MANUELA, *unable to bear more, turns to protest. Her mother gives her an owl-like wink.* MANUELA *suddenly has to control a laugh*) Lie down, Pedro, my darling. Sleep sweetly, my tired prince. Manuela,

fan him. (*She sticks the fan into* MANUELA'S *hand and covertly pokes her in the ribs.*)

PEDRO
(*Prone on the hammock*)

Go inside and shut up and take your no-good runt with you.

INES

Every word makes me see my daughter's perfidy. Poison in the sweet water. Seaweed in the scented air. Ah, my daughter—my daughter—cherish your blessing, lave his feet, worship the ground he treads so lightly. . . .

PEDRO
(*Shouts*)

I can't stand any more.

INES

You hear, Capucho, most unworthy of fathers, what your daughter has driven him to. Ah me! Alas and alack! (*To* PEDRO *as he tries vainly to sleep*) Dream of fields of clover, lovely one, and how much you can get for them! (*Beckons her husband*) Come, withered turnip. (*Very grandly she sweeps inside.* CAPUCHO *follows. He rattles.*)

PEDRO
(*Shouts*)

Don't rattle! (CAPUCHO *takes out cylinder, pours dice into his palm and in dumb-show offers to play.* PEDRO *becomes*

THE PIRATE

apoplectic) Play you! (CAPUCHO *nods*—PEDRO *shouts to* MA-
NUELA) He wants to play me! (*To* CAPUCHO) And if I win—
how will you pay?

CAPUCHO
(*Affably*)

You lend. (*He goes inside.* PEDRO *groans.*)

PEDRO

What a family! When your mother's tongue starts clacking,
it affects my heart.

MANUELA
(*Sits, hopeless*)

Well, rest then.

PEDRO

And no Isabellas when I wake?

MANUELA

No, husband.

PEDRO

And no tall ones?

MANUELA

No, and no short ones either!

PEDRO

Nothing.

MANUELA

Nothing, nothing at all . . . (*Groaning and grunting*,
PEDRO *stretches out on the hammock as we saw him at the*

opening of the scene. MANUELA *sits beside him, fans him slowly. He is soon snoring again. Tears well in* MANUELA'S *eyes.*)

FISHERBOY
(*Appears at window over* PEDRO'S *hammock*)
Donna Vargas!

MANUELA
Shh!

FISHERBOY
(*Holding up book*)
Does this belong to you? (*With a cry of joy* MANUELA *rises, and her finger goes instinctively to her lips to quiet the boy*) I was on the wharf fishing—it hits me on the head. I turned around and looked. . . .

PEDRO
(*Stirring*)
Robbers! (*At the sound of* PEDRO'S *voice, the* FISHERBOY'S *head disappears instantly, but he has thrown the book to* MANUELA. *She picks it up and hugs it to her*) Robbers! (PEDRO *turns over*) You'll hang for this! You'll hang!

MANUELA
He'll never hang!

PEDRO
You'll hang! (*Having disposed of his imaginary rival,* PEDRO *turns and sleeps deeply. Hugging the lost treasure to her,* MANUELA *sits beside her snoring husband. Her spirits are*

miraculously lifted. The return of the symbol has a seemingly disproportionate effect on her morale. She fans, she opens the book again, happily she settles herself to read, but after a moment she allows the book to fall into her lap. She daydreams aloud.)

MANUELA

Estramudo, where are you now? What horizon compasses you? What glow kindles in what horizon? Where you are, is it sunset or is it daybreak? Oh, return from afar, and save me—save Manuela. (*As she contemplates this impossible vision, there begins to throb from on high through the wavering mirage the music made by* SERAFIN's *Troupe as it works its way down the mountainside to the village square.* MANUELA *looks up, frightened. A mirage of the mind's eye she is used to, but a mirage of the ear is something new—something startling. Surely she must be dreaming this sound, and yet, there it is—louder, more insistent. Has she crossed too often the boundary of reality? Instinctively, in order to combat the sound from outside, she starts reading aloud to create her own reality against what she feels may be imagined*) "Above the flutes and cymbals, Estramudo, seated cross-legged beside his host, became aware of another sound . . ." (*But by this time the actual flutes and cymbals are too insistent to be ignored;* MANUELA *questions herself wildly. She looks up. Whence comes the music? It seems to recede. Does she hear it or does she not? She returns to the book, reading louder still*) . . . "a strange sweet singing, mournful-joyous, threaded through with the rhythm of muffled drums." (*She looks up again. She listens again. Flutes and drums. Surely these are flutes; these*

29

are drums. To make certain of her sanity she rises suddenly and calls for LIZARDA) Lizarda! (LIZARDA, MANUELA'S *maid, a lovely colored girl, comes in*) Lizarda . . .

LIZARDA

Yes, my lady.

MANUELA
(*Her eyes toward the music*)

Listen. . . .

LIZARDA

To what, lady?

MANUELA

Listen. . . .

LIZARDA

I'm listening powerful, my lady.

MANUELA

Do you hear what I hear?

LIZARDA

That affects what you hear, my lady.

MANUELA

Strange music—from the mountainside. . . .

LIZARDA

Oh, yes, lady—I hear that.

30

MANUELA

I thought I was going crazy. Is it voodoo?

LIZARDA

Oh, no, lady—that's not voodoo—that's foreign.

MANUELA
(*Relieved*)

That's what I thought. Listen—it's growing nearer, isn't it, Lizarda?

LIZARDA

Yes, it's sure coming nearer—it's coming down the mountainside as if . . .

MANUELA

Right down into the square . . .

LIZARDA

Right down into this very house, my lady. (LIZARDA *runs off to investigate.* MANUELA, *powerfully moved, returns to* PEDRO'S *hammock and stands beside it, fanning to the rhythm of the invading sound.*)

Curtain

ACT ONE

Scene II

Scene: *A mountain road winding down to the "saucer" in the hills, the village wherein sits the dreaming* MANUELA. *From this height the fiesta-garlanded village gleams and drowses in the afternoon sun.*

SERAFIN'S *Troupe, white and colored, incredibly weary and bedraggled but nevertheless making music, winds down the narrow road. The band is playing; snaredrum and flute, trumpets and guitar, even a hand-organ—all blare away for dear life.*

TRILLO, SERAFIN'S *colored aide-de-camp, enters first and points the way to the others as they appear.*

The troupe halts dejectedly. Several of them, more vociferously ESTABAN, *a white member, are in active mutiny.*

SEMPER
(*A colored member*)
My feet are complaining!

GUMBO
Complainin'? Mine are rebellin'! I can't control 'em no more. (*He falls down*) I accept their resignation. (*He collapses.*)

32

ESTABAN

Seems to me the distance from town to town is getting longer and longer and longer.

BOLO

Wish he could book us in the valleys. Seems we're always climbing mountains.

ESTABAN

The Captain sure finds towns that ain't even on the map. How does he discover them?

GUMBO

There's nothin' seems to discourage the boss. He always thinks the next town is good till we hits it.

SEMPER
(*Wearily*)

And there's always a next stand.

GUMBO

I wish we could get to a place where there is no next stand.

TRILLO
(*Pointing to the village below*)

Our next stand? There she is.

DON BOLO
(*Smoldering, rebellious*)

Stand after stand! Wish we could set and eat some place.

33

TRILLO

This is where our boss will turn the trick—I feel it in my bones.

ESTABAN

(*Open rebellion*)

He turns the trick all right, but what do you get out of it?

TRILLO

(*Loyally*)

You get what he gets—we share and share alike in this troupe.

ESTABAN

When you're sharing nothing, what difference does it make who gets the most?

TRILLO

Ain't you got no confidence in the future?

ESTABAN

That's the one thing I ain't got no confidence in.

TRILLO

Ain't you got no confidence in the boss?

ESTABAN

I'd have more confidence if he got us a square meal once in a while. I'm tired of dragging him around. Why don't he drag us for a change?

34

THE PIRATE

TRILLO

He's got to rest for his performance.

ESTABAN

Why don't we have to rest for ours?

TRILLO

Because he gives more than we do. That's why. Where's your courage gone to?

ESTABAN

You can't have courage when you don't eat.

DON BOLO
(Seized with a bright idea)

Trillo!

TRILLO
(Grandly)

Yes, Don Bolo. . . .

DON BOLO

Trillo *(His voice drops)*, do you know where he keeps the rabbit? *(His mouth watering)* I love stewed rabbit.

TRILLO
(Pretending ignorance)

What rabbit? Which?

ESTABAN

The rabbit he takes out of his kettle every night.

35

DON BOLO

Yes—let's get that rabbit.

TRILLO

That rabbit is an optical illusion. You can't eat no optical illusion.

DON BOLO

If it's an optical illusion, let him pull one out of the kettle right now and we go on.

TRILLO

That would be prostituting his art. That's for the public.

ESTABAN

Well, right now we're the public and that optical illusion is a live rabbit.

DON BOLO

Where's the rabbit?

DON BOLO

We eat or we don't go on.

ESTABAN *and* DON BOLO

Where's that rabbit?

TRILLO

I'm sworn to secrecy.

ESTABAN

Then I quit.

36

DON BOLO

So do I!

TRILLO

This is close to mutiny.

ESTABAN

Make the most of it.

TRILLO

I tell you this is the town where we hit the jackpot. He said so.

DON BOLO

He says it before every town.

ESTABAN

I'm quitting.

TRILLO

(*Appealing to his common sense*)

On this mountainside? What's the sense of that? Look how yonder village beckons. Give him this one more chance.

DON BOLO

If we don't eat this time, I go into the militia.

ESTABAN

That goes for me, Bolo. (*The others echo, "And for me," "And for me."*) And I'll tell him that when he wakes up.

37

THE PIRATE

All right, big mouth, tell him. Meantime we advance to the front. Squads up. . . . (*He marshals them forth. They follow him haltingly*) Forward! Courage, men. As the poet says, "Sic Semper Fidelis. Toujour de audacity." (*At this point, several members of the troupe lumber in, dragging the donkey cart on which, beneath a colored parasol, is piled the incredible paraphernalia of the troupe: props, magic effects, costumes and, bedded comfortably among these like a recumbent, parti-colored Crusader—invisible save for his crossed legs —dozes the master of the troupe himself. The donkey cart is propelled onward. . . .*)

Curtain

ACT ONE

SCENE III

SCENE: *The scene shifts over to the public square of the town. We now see the splendid house of* PEDRO VARGAS *and the neighboring house of the* WIDOW GALVEZ *in perspective. It is the siesta-hour; the square is droning with somnolence. The fisherboy we saw in Scene I is lying at the foot of the steps leading to* PEDRO'S *house, fast asleep. From a circular cavernous cellar-entrance below the bistro on the right comes the intermittent twang of a guitar strumming. The* HERMIT *is in there, he never comes out.*

In the far background the spires of the Cathedral shimmer in the heat. The great colored sails on the boats visible in the bay droop also; not a breeze stirring down there; in fact nothing is stirring anywhere.

The music of SERAFIN'S *Band begins to fill the square.* SERAFIN *and his troupe make their entrance.* SERAFIN, *now sitting up royally in the donkey-cart, is drawn in.* TRILLO *walks beside the cart.*

When the troupe reaches the center of the stage, SERAFIN *surveys the scene majestically; he jumps off the cart and dances with the troupe—a tantalizing sample of their art meant to entice the populace, but nothing happens. No one appears except* LIZARDA, *who sticks her head out of the door,*

39

takes one look and quickly shuts the door. A few windows close. SERAFIN *draws from his troupe three great drum rolls; the last one is quite imperious. Nevertheless absolutely nothing happens—not a stir. The troupe gives up in discouragement. They lie down in attitudes of despair, except* SERAFIN, *who addresses them as if he had just achieved a triumph.*

SERAFIN

(*The Emperor surveying the terrain in advance of conquest*)
Are we in the heart of the city?

TRILLO

The heart's stopped.

SERAFIN

(*Majestically, he steps out of the cart*)
We shall galvanize it!

ESTABAN

What did I tell you?

SERAFIN

What are artists for?

TRILLO

To go hungry.

SERAFIN

It is a challenge. Behold this village—a catalepsy. The power of art shall transform the paralytic into a dervish-dancer. We shall lubricate this community.

TRILLO

We can't lubricate our own stomachs. . . . All these towns seem to shrink up when we hit them.

BOLO

We stimulate the outgoing traffic.

TRILLO

Oh, what's the use?

BOLO

Trillo's right. What's the use?

SERAFIN

(*Menacing*)

What did you say, Don Bolo?

DON BOLO

Trillo's right. What's the use?

SERAFIN

Gentlemen, I must remind you of the dignity of our calling. We are artists. As such it is our duty to be irrepressible. If I, the descendant on one side of the immortal playwright, Lope de Vega, and his sometime mistress—that Queen who commissioned Columbus to discover new lands—if I, in whom flows the blood of the poet and purest Castilian, if I, Serafin, can withstand these slings and arrows, cannot you, who are made of baser metal, shuffle them off? I pause. . . . (*There is a sullen silence.*)

DON BOLO

You're descended from nothing!

SERAFIN

(*Patient, cold*)

Do I understand you correctly, Don Bolo? Do you impugn my veracity?

DON BOLO

No, I don't do that. I jes say you're a God-awful liar! (*The others are a bit shocked at this blasphemy though they have for some time privately shared it. A silence.* SERAFIN *towers above* DON BOLO.)

SERAFIN

(*Quietly*)

Repeat that remark, Don Bolo.

DON BOLO

I ain't no Don. You call us all Don.

SERAFIN

(*Patiently*)

As one of royal blood, it is my prerogative to confer titles.

DON BOLO

But I ain't no Don. I'm jes Bolo.

SERAFIN

(*With impeccable dignity*)

I can see that by ennobling you I have ennobled the unworthy. In other circumstances, I should have you quietly garroted. However, in this case—noblesse oblige—my last cigar. Pass it among the boys. (BOLO *grabs the cigar with avidity.* SERAFIN *eyes the sleeping* FISHERBOY, *approaches him, touches him lightly with his foot to wake him.*)

SERAFIN
(*To* FISHERBOY)
Forgive me, young man, forgive me. But we are artists.

BOY
(*Unmoved*)
I can't help that!

SERAFIN
We wish to give a performance here. Where do we get a license?

BOY
You can't get no license.

SERAFIN
(*Haughty*)
And why not, pray?

BOY
Because the Censor won't give you one nohow. All acting folk hotfoot it through this town. Don Pedro don't like 'em.

SERAFIN
And who is this Don Pedro who deigns to dislike us?

43

BOY

He's de riches' man in town.

SERAFIN

And where does this bigoted Nabob reside?

BOY

(*Over his shoulder*)

Right there.

SERAFIN

Smug residence! (*The* FISHERBOY *goes off*) Bundle of nerves, isn't he? (*To* TRILLO) Trillo . . .

TRILLO

Yes, Captain.

SERAFIN

Ring the doorbell of that mansion. Apprise the flunky that Serafin of Madrid presents his compliments and wishes to see the Censor.

TRILLO

To what avail?

SERAFIN

What!

TRILLO

My behind is dislocated from the last time I presented your compliments.

SERAFIN

(*Grandly*)

The condition of your posterior does not interest me. I order you to ring that doorbell! (*From the semi-circular opening of the cellar entrance below the bistro the* HERMIT *starts twanging a melancholy but persuasive tune.* SERAFIN *is struck by it*) No, wait, Trillo—wait. A sign of life already. It's good! Something to purloin. Purloin it, boys. (*The boys pick it up on their instruments.* SERAFIN *darts to the crescent opening. Between cupped hands he calls down to the* HERMIT) Who dwells within?

HERMIT

One who seeks solitude.

SERAFIN

Want to earn two pesos? (TRILLO *laughs ironically at this fantastically impossible offer.*)

HERMIT

No.

SERAFIN

Why not?

HERMIT

Money corrupts.

SERAFIN

Then I shall give you nothing. But come out.

HERMIT

Not for anything.

SERAFIN

Why not?

HERMIT

Humanity corrupts.

SERAFIN

A philosopher! The town has quality! We should prosper here.

TRILLO

(*With a glance around, sadly*)
I lack your consanguinity.

SERAFIN

Don't be defeatist, Trillo. Art is optimism.

TRILLO

We were so bereft in our last stop we had to dispose of our donkey. How do you inspire yourself?

SERAFIN

Don't ask me to explain the mystery of genius. (ISABELLA *swings in. She gives* SERAFIN *the eye.* SERAFIN *gives her a magnificent bow. To* ISABELLA) Gracious lady.

ISABELLA

(*Stopping center and turning*)
Players?

SERAFIN

For your delight, we hope.

46

ISABELLA

I'm sorry for your sake. There's not much of a public in this village.

SERAFIN

Your presence, gracious lady, refutes that. Does it not contain you?

ISABELLA

A pretty wit. Where does it come from?

SERAFIN

That other universe—my spirit.

ISABELLA

What's your name?

SERAFIN

My true name is long and complicated and crusted with tradition. Call me Serafin. And gracious lady—yours?

ISABELLA

Isabella.

SERAFIN

An omen!

ISABELLA

A good omen, I hope.

SERAFIN

Another Isabella was an ancestor of mine.

ISABELLA

(*Sarcastically*)

The Queen, I suppose!

SERAFIN

Your intuition matches your beauty. (*She smiles at him*)
We give a performance tonight.

ISABELLA

You'll give no performance in this town.

SERAFIN

Why not? We are here.

ISABELLA

You can't give a performance without a license.

SERAFIN

A formality—a stroke of the pen.

ISABELLA

You can only get it from old Pedro Vargas.

SERAFIN

And he?

ISABELLA

He's inhospitable to strangers. Those who have any dealings
with him whatever often cast doubt on his legitimacy.

48

SERAFIN

I should think the accident of his birth would make him sympathize with the unexpected.

ISABELLA

(*Laughs. Points to* MANUELA's *house*)
See that balcony. . . .

SERAFIN

Juliet's balcony . . .

ISABELLA
(*Sardonic*)
Where Juliet's petticoat hangs by yonder washline . . .

SERAFIN
(*Struck*)

A new idea!

ISABELLA

A new idea for what?

SERAFIN

When I play Romeo—I shall festoon the balcony with clotheslines. It will satisfy the intelligentsia who clamor for realism! All I ask of you is to introduce me to the Censor. I'll undertake to do the rest.

ISABELLA

He hates me. I corrupt his wife. I give her books to read.
(LIZARDA *appears in* MANUELA's *doorway*.)

SERAFIN

He must be taught a lesson, this reactionary.

LIZARDA

Did you ring our bell, sir?

ISABELLA

Oh, Lizarda . . .

LIZARDA

Please, Señora!

ISABELLA

What's the matter with you?

LIZARDA

My master has forbidden me to converse with you. I dis-recognize you.

ISABELLA

Oh, you do, eh? (TRILLO *by this time is lost in his adoration of* LIZARDA. *He gazes at her lovingly, all during this scene.*)

LIZARDA

Please do not embarrass me.

ISABELLA

You see, I'm not good enough to speak to their maid, and my husband—rest his soul—was an alderman!

LIZARDA

Please, Señora!

ISABELLA
(*Starting down steps*)
I've a good mind to blacken that pretty little eye of yours!

SERAFIN
No vandalism, gracious lady. She's a sweet girl.

LIZARDA
Thank you, sir.

SERAFIN
Tell your master that Serafin of Madrid wishes to see him.
It is important and immediate!

LIZARDA
I shall be glad to apprise him, sir. (*She goes in.*)

SERAFIN
(*Admonishing* TRILLO)
Trillo, Trillo. Oh, in the spring, in the spring . . . (*To*
ISABELLA) In the spring, a girl is a wonderful thing, in the
spring . . . Are you free this evening?

ISABELLA
I could be, though I had promised two lieutenants . . .

SERAFIN
Bring them to my performance tonight.

ISABELLA

There'll be no performance. That leaves you free, doesn't it? I could be free too. (PEDRO *comes out on his little porch and watches them.*)

SERAFIN

But the two lieutenants would be devastated.

ISABELLA

They're new recruits.

SERAFIN

Happy pupils!

PEDRO

(*Bursting in—to* ISABELLA)

You've found your level, I see.

ISABELLA

(*With a devastating smile at* SERAFIN)

I hope so. (*She goes out.*)

PEDRO

Well, mountebank . . . ?

SERAFIN

I am Serafin of Madrid.

PEDRO

So I've heard.

THE PIRATE

SERAFIN

I am a stranger in your city. . . .

PEDRO

You will remain so.

SERAFIN

I am an artist. These gentlemen (*He indicates his troupe, drooping in the back. The players stiffen up and bow*) are artists also. We are masters of many skills, of song and of speech. I tell the past, present and future. We wish to give a performance here. Will you, as the town's first citizen—will you be our patron?

PEDRO

(*Dumbfounded at the request*)

Your patron!

SERAFIN

Will you so win a modest immortality?

PEDRO

Ten minutes!

SERAFIN

My lord?

PEDRO

I give you and your malodorous riffraff there exactly ten minutes to get out of town.

SERAFIN

My lord!

THE PIRATE

PEDRO

I am not a lord. I am a hard-headed business man. Flattery won't get you anywhere with me.

SERAFIN

My lord, I shall be under no pretense with you. We are artists. We are children. But fame has not yet touched us, not even lightly. Are we to be exiled for that? Look at my aide-de-camp, Trillo—his songs express a naive delight in sheer existence. Bolo juggles marvelously. Sambo strums a guitar and sets the feet to dancing. For a moment he will quicken the slow rhythm of your lives. Give us this moment. For, unless we perform, we do not live. Do not imprison our skills. Let us express ourselves for this one night and then we go our way.

PEDRO

Ten minutes!

SERAFIN

What, sir? (*Gradually, with accumulating and tantalizing force, something about* PEDRO *starts clamping on* SERAFIN *a gnawing pincer of memory. He stares at him. He withdraws from him. He stares at him from a farther perspective. He starts, in a wide arc, to encircle him.*)

PEDRO

I give you exactly ten minutes to get out of this town. This is a respectable community. We do not entertain the scum of the cities. It is to get away from such as you that we live here. When I opened my window just now I sniffed in the wind a whiff of corruption. I see now what it is. You and your starvelings! Get out, do you hear? Ten minutes to get out. Ten minutes!

SERAFIN

Speak more, master, speak more. . . .

PEDRO

I'll have you in jail. And it's a mean jail. As lousy as you are.

SERAFIN

Speak—speak . . .

PEDRO

What's the matter with you? Epilepsy?

SERAFIN

No, I am dreaming. I am dreaming—no.

PEDRO

Ten minutes to get out—you and your troupe. Ten minutes. (SERAFIN *leaps up on top of the cart. His troupe huddle around. From behind* PEDRO, *with startling suddenness, comes a voice, seemingly out of the air. It says loudly, clearly:*)

THE VOICE

Mene Mene Tekel Upharsin. (SERAFIN *and his troupe echo this voice in an eerie ululation. This vocal apparition has an extraordinary effect on* PEDRO. *He jumps as if shot. He grows pale. He clutches his heart. Beads of perspiration stand out on his forehead.*)

PEDRO
(*Agonized*)
Merciful Mother of God!

SERAFIN
(*In a terrible voice*)
Indeed, my lord Pedro, the handwriting on the wall!

PEDRO
Merciful Mother . . .

SERAFIN
(*In the same voice*)
The Devil is dying, my lord Pedro. The devil is dying. (*Pantherlike and commanding now, he addresses the troupe*) Gentlemen—deploy!

TRILLO
(*Military attention*)
Where to, north or south? East or west?

SERAFIN
Publicize our performance this evening.

BOLO
What's the use publicizing what ain't gonna be?

SERAFIN
Leave that to me.

56

THE PIRATE

ESTABAN

We've left it to you till the starvation point.

SERAFIN

One more act of faith.

BOLO

All right, but it's the last act.

SERAFIN

Do as I say, Trillo.

TRILLO

(*Obedience is instant; saluting*)

Your word, Captain, is my law. (SERAFIN *and* PEDRO *are left alone. Trembling,* PEDRO *crosses himself.*)

PEDRO

(*Shattered*)

Where was it—did I hear it?

SERAFIN

Would you like to hear it again?

PEDRO

No, no! Are you the Devil? Are you the Devil?

SERAFIN

(*Jumping down and coming close to* PEDRO *to accuse him*)

He is much nearer, I think, to you—Estramudo.

THE PIRATE

PEDRO

(In a paralysis of panic)

Shh—for the sake of . . .

SERAFIN

Truly it's the incredible that always comes to pass. My, you've changed. You've become respectable, Estramudo.

PEDRO

I beg you—I beg you . . .

SERAFIN

What are you doing here? Doesn't it bore you? After all those years on the seven seas! Doesn't it bore you, after murder and torture, and drowning, and booty—endless booty? What do you do evenings, Estramudo?

PEDRO

Merciful Mother of God!

SERAFIN

All I ask is a license for our show—that's a small price for silence, Estramudo.

PEDRO

Don't say that name.

SERAFIN

My, my, but you've put on weight. When we last met—you were lithe—you were strong.

PEDRO

You did it! When you captured me. That made me turn
over a new leaf. If you hadn't been on that ship! How did
you come to be there?

SERAFIN

I was returning from Algiers where I had just fulfilled,
with resounding success—I may say—a professional engagement.

PEDRO

When I attacked your ship.

SERAFIN

We gave you a strong fight, Estramudo.

PEDRO

Sh . . .

SERAFIN

You were about to decapitate our officer. My voice from
an unexpected quarter—Mene . . .

PEDRO

Sh . . .

SERAFIN

Tell me, why did that mystical abracadabra frighten you
so?

PEDRO

(*Pitifully*)

I'm superstitious!

59

SERAFIN

That's putting it mildly. . . . You were terrified.

PEDRO

It was that sound that came from nowhere—that terrible sound.

SERAFIN

It's one of our best effects. What's the matter with it?

PEDRO

I heard that sound once before in Baghdad, when I was condemned to die. I associate it with the call of the muezzin —the muezzin of death.

SERAFIN

Really!

PEDRO

How did you know it? How?

SERAFIN

I don't give away any professional secrets, but in confidence I will tell you this—I am the seventh son of a seventh son, and born with a veil. It is rumored that Cagliastro was my father. I am the only child in recorded history ever to be lifted from the caul by levitation. Now you tell me something? I was going to share the reward with the captain; he had you safely below decks in chains. How did you escape?

PEDRO

Bribery.

SERAFIN

But you had nothing on you. We'd searched you thoroughly.

PEDRO

I swallowed two rubies.

SERAFIN

Luxurious diet. And since?

PEDRO

I'd had enough. I came here with my capital.

SERAFIN
(*Ironically*)

Whose capital?

PEDRO

My capital. Are you a communist?

SERAFIN

No. No. And then?

PEDRO

As you see. Quiet life. Regular meals. Philanthropy.

SERAFIN

Don't you miss the old life?

61

PEDRO

I hate it. I loathe it. I never thought of it till now. But you can't prove it. You can't prove anything. Remember that. (SERAFIN *bursts out laughing. He laughs uncontrollably*) What are you laughing at?

SERAFIN

So this is Estramudo, the legendary! This is the terror of the seven seas! The novelist's gold-mine, the poet's inspiration —you!

PEDRO

If you denounce me, I'll say you're crazy. I'll have you locked up.

SERAFIN

Do we get the license?

PEDRO
(*Turns, starts to walk away*)

No!

SERAFIN
(*Singing*)

Mene, Mene, Tekel Upharsin. . . .

PEDRO
(*As though kicked in stomach*)

Don't do that!

SERAFIN

Do we get it?

PEDRO

For one performance. On condition you get out right after.

SERAFIN

I have no wish to remain here, Estramudo. My desire for respectability is not as great as yours.

PEDRO

But it's understood—you leave immediately after the performance tonight.

SERAFIN
(*Again overcome with laughter*)
Estramudo, the Censor! I can't bear it. (PEDRO *starts across the stage*) Where are you going, Prince of Pirates?

PEDRO
(*Wiping his brow, crosses himself*)
To Mass! (*He exits in the direction of the Cathedral.* SERA-FIN *watches him off, divinely amused. He is in terrific fettle. He looks around him, at the Square, at the houses. Somehow he feels that this little square will be for him a gladiatorial arena from which he will emerge victorious.* TRILLO *shambles back.*)

SERAFIN
(*Improvising to himself*)
Ladies and Gentlemen. At the especial request of the Alcalde, Don Pedro . . . Hello, Trillo.

TRILLO

Hello, Captain. I've publicized my head off, but my pronouncements has been received with skepticism.

SERAFIN

Tonight, Trillo, marks the turn of our fortunes.

TRILLO

(*With admiration*)

That's what makes you a nacherl leader, Captain. You're more than jes sanguine, you're contagious.

SERAFIN

Distribute handbills—to this effect: Tonight our performance takes place under the patronage of the Alcalde Don Pedro Vargas himself.

TRILLO

(*Amazed*)

Shu nuff!

SERAFIN

Sure as spring, my Trillo.

TRILLO

(*Not quite convinced*)

Where do you get that certitude?

SERAFIN

There are days when I feel within myself an accretion of such power that the impossible becomes a pushover. This is

one of those days! (MANUELA *comes out of her house. She
wears a lovely Spanish costume. She looks exquisite. She carries a reticule and a parasol. She puts up her parasol; the
two stare at her.* TRILLO *emits a long, admiring whistle and
exits.* MANUELA *starts across the stage, moving demurely.* SERA-
FIN *starts a concentric circling of her. She finds herself facing
him. The few musicians in the neighborhood tinkle a sympathetic obligato to this scene for a while.*)

SERAFIN
(*Finally*)
Are you a maiden? (*She stops, startled, does not look at
him. His voice trembling*) For me it is as vital as a heartbeat
to know.

MANUELA
(*Icily crisp*)
In Madrid, I hear, the ladies do not walk without their
duennas. Must we introduce that custom into this hitherto
peaceful village? Here at least I should have thought body-
guards were unnecessary.

SERAFIN
Were you to walk the lonely spaces of the Sahara, the dim
fields of the lost, described by Dante, were the universe all
but extinct, some ultimate spark of life there would kindle
dangerously as you passed. You, gracious lady, will always
need a bodyguard. From the boatman of the Styx, from
Charon himself. Do not look at him. Do not catch his eye.
He will scuttle his ferry.

MANUELA
(*After a moment*)
You are very extravagant.

SERAFIN
Do not lengthen my suspense. Who are you?

MANUELA
I am a wife. (*At this horrific announcement, the music stops.*)

SERAFIN
(*Affronted, angry*)
Then you should never step into the sight of other men. It is a provocation not to be endured.

MANUELA
I shall remove the provocation. (*She starts to move on.* SERAFIN *is struck by a horrid thought.*)

SERAFIN
Wait. No—no—it can't be! That would be too grotesque. Oh, gracious lady, tell me that isn't true.

MANUELA
I do not know what it is you wish me to deny—but if it will make you feel better if I do deny it, then I see no reason why I shouldn't. Have it your own way. Whatever it is—it is not true. Good day, Señor. (*She starts on, but she finds him again before her.*)

SERAFIN

Not him. Of all men in the world, not him.

MANUELA

Very well. Not him. Not him.

SERAFIN
(*In agony*)

Yes. It is he—it is he. . . .

MANUELA

You vacillate so.

SERAFIN

You're not married to *him*—not to that mountainous . . .

MANUELA
(*Very cold, imperious*)

Don Pedro Vargas is my husband and you will do well
not to malign him or his wrath may be turned upon you, to
say nothing of mine.

SERAFIN

His wrath upon me!

MANUELA

He is an amiable friend, but a vindictive enemy.

SERAFIN
(*His voice rises*)

What of my wrath against him!

67

MANUELA

Now, what can you possibly have against my husband?

SERAFIN

He defies the eternal principle of the rightness of things. It is a personal affront.

MANUELA

You're insane.

SERAFIN

If he had had any fastidiousness, he would have known that you were not for him. He would have stood aside.

MANUELA
(*Amused now*)

For you, I suppose?

SERAFIN

For someone aware of what you are.

MANUELA

Like you, for instance.

SERAFIN
(*Tensely*)

Yes.

MANUELA

Aren't you expecting too much of him? After all—he's not clairvoyant.

SERAFIN

Neither a sense of his future, nor a memory of his past.
Neither sight nor sense. Neither feeling nor scruple.

MANUELA

You know him?

SERAFIN

Yes, I know him.

MANUELA

You are impertinent then to speak so of him. I will not
listen. Good day. Now let me pass.

SERAFIN
(*Dreamily*)

On the other hand, I should be grateful . . .

MANUELA

You should be grateful that he allows you to enter this
village.

SERAFIN

If he had stood aside and another had come—the discrep-
ancy might be less marked, and my suit more hopeless.

MANUELA
(*Taunting him*)

It's a suit, is it?

SERAFIN
(*Quietly*)

It is a suit which I shall pursue to its end. (*Calmly*) Hence-

69

forth, all my thoughts will be of you. My longings sluiced now in one deep current of desire. What is your name?

MANUELA

Donna Vargas.

SERAFIN

No, not his name—your name.

MANUELA

Manuela . . .

SERAFIN

Manuela!

MANUELA

Now, please let me go. You're very entertaining. I like you. You're nice—a little flamboyant, perhaps—and certainly not well balanced—but nice—and I'm not at all sure you're sincere, but whether you are or not, you're nice. Now, please let me go. . . .

SERAFIN

Where do you go?

MANUELA

(*Laughing a little at herself, walks away—he walks beside her*) I go to a quiet little place I know of by the sea—to read.

SERAFIN

To read! (*He takes hold of her parasol as if to help her and presently she relinquishes it so that he finds himself holding it over her.*)

MANUELA

(*Explaining breathlessly*)

Yes. You see, at home I get no chance whatever to read. My husband's a very fine man!

SERAFIN

A very generous man.

MANUELA

Oh, I love him dearly—but he's something of a hypochondriac and I have to watch him—like a—sentinel—for symptoms. Then there are the servants and household decisions and callers. . . .

SERAFIN

Your husband is quite a prominent man?

MANUELA

Quite the most prominent in the village, you might say—and the house is always full of people. . . .

SERAFIN

And so you have to run away.

MANUELA

Yes, at the moment my husband is at Mass. Oh, he's very religious.

SERAFIN

I'm sure!

MANUELA

Oh, he's admirable in every way.

SERAFIN

A paragon, isn't he?

MANUELA

Yes, you could call him a paragon. (*She walks away from him and starts down the steps, but he darts around and meets her as she reaches the foot of the steps*) You'll never get anywhere with me by deprecating him. In fact it rather puts me off. (*As he confronts her suddenly*) We do meet so often lately.

SERAFIN

I don't deprecate him. Of all men in the world, I think he is the most enviable.

MANUELA

Thank you. You do pay pretty compliments. If you know him, perhaps he'll invite you to tea and then we could meet under more . . .

SERAFIN

Proper auspices.

MANUELA

Yes. I see you understand. Good day, Señor. (*She starts off.*)

SERAFIN

(*Stopping her again*)

When you get to your little retreat—what is it you read?

72

MANUELA

Oh, I'm afraid you'd think it rather silly. My husband does.

SERAFIN

Then it's possible I will consider it profound.

MANUELA

I'm reading the sayings of Marcus Aurelius.

SERAFIN

(*Skeptically*)

The sayings of Marcus Aurelius. . . . I don't believe you.
. . . Show me what you read.

MANUELA

(*Taking out* ESTRAMUDO's *book*)

Well, at the moment I am reading this one. Have you read
it? (*She gives him the book. He opens it, looks at it, looks
at her. He looks at her sharply. Is she having him on? Is it
conceivable that she is innocent? Warily, he questions her.*)

SERAFIN

Do you know this man?

MANUELA

Know him—Estramudo! Marooned here as I am, how
could I know him?

SERAFIN

Have you ever seen him?

MANUELA

Oh, yes—often!

SERAFIN

You've seen him often!

MANUELA

In my mind's eye.

SERAFIN

Oh, only there?

MANUELA

How else? Where else?

SERAFIN

What is there about this man that seizes your imagination?

MANUELA

(*Clasps book to her bosom, quietly, starry-eyed*)
He transcends reality.

SERAFIN

And what good does that do you?

MANUELA

What good? How prosaic! You sound like Pedro.

SERAFIN

Oh, no. I have wild dreams about myself also, but they're

74

extensions of myself. I never substitute another hero for my-self—especially one as remote as this Estramudo must be to you.

MANUELA

He is not remote. He is near to me. I live with him.

SERAFIN

You live with him!

MANUELA

Figuratively speaking. . . . (*He circles her, he feels his mind reeling a bit*) I do wish you'd stop circling around me like that—it's like talking to a top.

SERAFIN

You bewilder me.

MANUELA

I'm a hero-worshiper. I once had a crush on Napoleon. My aunt knew him. She grew up with him in Corsica. I sent him some fruit once to St. Helena.

SERAFIN

Did he acknowledge it?

MANUELA
(*Sadly*)

No, he never did.

SERAFIN

But would you send fruit to an outlaw with a price on his head?

MANUELA

Don't be a prude! These little ethical straitjackets can't hold in a man like Estramudo. . . .

SERAFIN

No, that's true—they can't!

MANUELA

On the moving waters he darts about, this dragon-fly of the seas, glittering and uncapturable. In bold strokes, like a fresco of Michael Angelo, he has slashed across the world the great pattern of his imaginations, a superb design of adventure for men to marvel and wonder at.

SERAFIN

You are in love with this man?

MANUELA

In a way.

SERAFIN

But what if you knew him?

MANUELA

The question is academic.

SERAFIN

But if you did—if you met him . . . ?

MANUELA

It would depend a bit on what he looked like, wouldn't it? His manners? After all, he personally might be quite disenchanting—even a bore. How do I know?

SERAFIN

Well, you're the most extraordinary mixture of fantasy and realism it has ever been my good fortune to encounter.

MANUELA

Am I? I don't think so. There is the practical world and the world of the imagination. I know which is which. I don't mix them.

SERAFIN

I don't agree. If your imagination doesn't bring reality, then it's a mere lie—a mere delusion.

MANUELA

You're a pragmatist. To me imagination is just an escape. The less it has to do with reality the better. That is its essence.

SERAFIN

What I mean is this. As we sit here together, side by side, my mind leaps forward to that moment, to that marvelous moment . . .

77

MANUELA

Please do not leap. It will do you no good to leap. I am a married woman.

SERAFIN

That seems to be your slogan.

MANUELA

My husband is very kind to me, and I do hope I have a sense of fair play.

SERAFIN

A Lorelei with a conscience! For a woman so addicted to the niceties of equity you certainly pick peculiar heroes.

MANUELA

Perhaps that's why I pick them as remote from myself as possible. Good day, Señor. Oh, dear—I've talked to you for so long now, I'm afraid I'll have no time left to read. (*She gets up, forgetting her parasol, and starts toward her house. But again she finds herself confronted by* SERAFIN) You do get about in the oddest way!

SERAFIN

But if he were not?

MANUELA

If he were not what?

SERAFIN

This Estramudo, if you met him—and he were personally

on a par with his deeds—not a bore at all—took his career for granted—never mentioned it, in fact—were entertaining, fascinating—even lovable on his own . . .

MANUELA

Oh, dear!

SERAFIN

(*Insisting passionately*)

What then?

MANUELA

That might be difficult to resist.

SERAFIN

But you would try?

MANUELA

I should succeed.

SERAFIN

You are sure of yourself!

MANUELA

Yes.

SERAFIN

But why? Why?

MANUELA

Fair play.

SERAFIN

I see.

MANUELA
(*Laughs*)

You see, do you?

SERAFIN

Don't laugh at me.

MANUELA

If I didn't laugh, I should be annoyed with you. Now please let me pass.

SERAFIN

Never.

MANUELA

Don't be silly. . . .

SERAFIN

I love you. And love is not silly.

MANUELA
(*Soberly, analytically*)

No. Love is not silly. But most of the prattle about it is. Now please let me go.

SERAFIN

You don't believe me?

MANUELA

If you had met Isabella there you would have said it to her.

SERAFIN

I did meet her.

MANUELA
(*A little piqued*)

Oh. . . .

SERAFIN

And I made a rendezvous with her—somewhat elastic. . . .

MANUELA

Oh, you did. . . .

SERAFIN

But I did not say it to her.

MANUELA
(*Trying to pass*)

Good-bye.

SERAFIN

Shall I prove that I love you?

MANUELA

Love is not a problem in geometry. How can you prove it?

SERAFIN

I can prove it—by putting my life in your hands. . . .

MANUELA

Why should you do that?

SERAFIN

Because I want it there.

MANUELA

What would I do with it?

SERAFIN

What you will.

MANUELA

It's a responsibility. It's sweet of you. But thank you, no.

SERAFIN

You're not curious?

MANUELA

(*In spite of herself*)

Who are you anyway?

SERAFIN

If I tell you—the responsibility will be yours already. Can you bear it?

MANUELA

You're very strange.

SERAFIN

Stranger even than your dreams. . . .

MANUELA

(*Drawn in against her will*)

Who are you?

SERAFIN

(*In a whisper*)

I am the stuff of your dreams materialized. I am he about

whom your imagination plays. I am—I am Estramudo the
Pirate. (*There is a long pause. She looks at him.*)

MANUELA

You said just now that I was a mixture of fantasy and
realism. I am now in my mood of realism.

SERAFIN

You don't believe me?

MANUELA

(*After a moment. She half does*)

No.

SERAFIN

You know it to be true.

MANUELA

(*Playing for time*)

So you think you are presentable, do you?

SERAFIN

This disguise is hardly becoming. You should see me
dressed up.

MANUELA

Fascinating—even lovable!

SERAFIN

Oh, don't turn my words against me, Manuela. . . .

MANUELA

Why not?

SERAFIN

When I spoke them I had no idea of revealing my identity to you.

MANUELA

I think where women are concerned you are pretty calculating. Keep your engagement with Isabella. (MANUELA *opens the door quickly and slams it in his face. He finds himself alone. He tries the door. It is locked. He tries it harder. It is definitely locked. We hear the staccato drumming of* SERAFIN'S *troupe—a droning vibration punctured in regular, insistent rhythm. He withdraws, looks at* MANUELA'S *house, at* ISABELLA'S *house—surveying the terrain.* TRILLO *comes back. After him straggle other members of the troupe, including the band.*)

TRILLO

(*Very excited*)

Captain, Captain! I have pontificated our performance and there is a certain interest.

SERAFIN

(*Still looking up at* MANUELA'S *balcony*)

Good, Trillo!

BOLO

It's more than an interest—it's an apprehension.

TRILLO

We shall gratify it!

84

THE PIRATE

BOLO

It's the first show since Don Pedro has been the Alcalde.

TRILLO

They think as the Alcalde allows it, it must be good. We have the great virtue of novelty.

BOLO

Maybe we'll even be able to buy a couple of fish.

SERAFIN
(Snaps out of his revery—the man of action again)
After tonight, my hearties, there will be a plentitude of fish. Set for the show, boys.

TRILLO
(A little surprised)
Right here? In the residential quarter? It's more crowded up the hill.

SERAFIN

The crowd will come to us, Trillo. Not we to the crowd.

TRILLO

That has not been our experience so far.

SERAFIN
(Taking TRILLO *aside)*
Trillo, you saw that lady there . . .

TRILLO

Yes, Captain.

SERAFIN

She has a maid.

TRILLO

We have exchanged glances.

SERAFIN

To her I want you to convey that I am not Serafin the Player at all but Estramudo the Pirate. (*To* BOLO) Bolo, that rope will do very well to hang our props on. (*He indicates the clothesline on* MANUELA's *balcony.* BOLO *grabs it and trails it over to* SERAFIN.)

TRILLO
(*Stunned*)

Estramudo the Pirate!

SERAFIN

Can I entrust this to you?

TRILLO
(*Aghast*)

But that's fraught with peril, Captain. Suppose she distributes it?

SERAFIN

I want her to. I want her to tell it all over town.

TRILLO

Oh, Captain, you've got me all confused.

86

SERAFIN

Leave the strategy to me. You be the executant.

TRILLO

If they catch me—I'll sure be the executant.

SERAFIN

(*He eyes the space between the two houses*)
Trust me, Trillo, trust me.

TRILLO

Your wish is my desire.

SERAFIN

Now then. (*He takes* MANUELA's *rope from* BOLO.)

ESTABAN

Gonna do the rope trick tonight, Captain?

SERAFIN

May go back to my iron-jaw act. Tonight, boys, we must be good. . . . We must. (*Testing rope*) Oh, this will do excellently; it will do very well indeed. (*Hands rope to* TRILLO *and crosses to the trellis leading up to* ISABELLA's *balcony. To the musicians:*) Give me a roll and a chord in G. (*He does a knee bend and starts climbing trellis*) Bolo, my boy, I may chop you in two tonight.

BOLO

(*Reminiscently*)

You ain't chopped me in a long time, Captain.

SERAFIN

(*As he climbs*)

We're going to do a lot of things tonight that we haven't done in a long time.

BOLO

(*To* TRILLO)

The thermometer sure is rising! I ain't ever seen him climb for it before. Lucky the lady is a widow, eh, Trillo?

TRILLO

(*Loftily*)

I don't hold with such petty gossip. Besides, the boss's lady don't live in this house— (*Pointing to* ISABELLA'S) she lives in that house. (*Pointing to* MANUELA'S. *By this time* SERAFIN *is on* ISABELLA'S *balcony, tying the rope to the railing and facing* MANUELA'S *house.*)

SERAFIN

(*Addressing the Universe*)

From this house to that house—from the profane to the sacred—from the body to the spirit—from earth to heaven— (*Suddenly the vision strikes him—he sees the stretched rope— a straight rope to* MANUELA'S *bedroom*) Oh, oho, I wish—I wish . . . !

THE PIRATE

TRILLO

(*Apprehensive*)

What's wrong, Captain? Scared of the height?

SERAFIN

No, I eat the air, promise-crammed . . . (*He takes off his shoes.*)

TRILLO

Are you dizzy, Captain?

SERAFIN

Yes, I'm dizzy. Throw me that umbrella. (TRILLO *tosses* MANUELA's *parasol up to him*) I'm dizzy with the singing of angels—I'm dizzy with the choirs of heaven. (*His men think he has gone crazy, they are worried*) It's a road to heaven— a straight and narrow road to heaven. (SERAFIN *starts walking the tight-rope to* MANUELA's *balcony.*)

BOLO

He's gettin' religion! He's goin' to heaven! (*In an ecstasy the troupe starts clapping its hands and improvising a rousing spiritual as* SERAFIN, *balancing with* MANUELA's *parasol, walks the improvised tight-rope. The song and the rhythm mount and mount as* SERAFIN *teeters crazily on the clothesline. Partly for the sake of those actors who are not congenital tight-rope walkers, a "transparency curtain" may descend (as, in fact, it does on the current production of this play!), a curtain obligingly cut so as to minimize the risk for the perilously peri-*

patetic SERAFIN. *We see his head, his arms and shoulders diz-*
zily balancing with MANUELA'S *parasol: painted on the curtain*
Reubens-like, beneficent colored angels, their arms raised in
supplication, help him on his way; the troupe sings him on;
the God Eros guides him. . . .

Curtain

ACT TWO

ACT TWO

SCENE: MANUELA's *bedroom: lavishly baroque; green and yellow; a great, heavily pillared canopy bed, an ornate fortress. On the right, a tall, French window, curtained, which leads out onto the balcony. It is to this balcony that* SERAFIN *has improvised his highway from* ISABELLA's *balcony.*

The action is overlapping. We hear the singing and the shouting that, at the end of the first act, accompany SERAFIN's *maneuver.*

INES *and* CAPUCHO *are shooting craps. She is playing and talking and winning. She has been winning for some time.* CAPUCHO *is miserable, gaunt and resentful. He plays desperately, trying to get a break under the barrage of his wife's chatter. They are on their hands and knees on the floor.*

INES
(As CAPUCHO *rolls)*

Ah, four! Come on, come on—better luck next time, beloved mummy. *(She is impatient, waiting for* CAPUCHO *to roll when music is heard through the window)* What is that? A serenade? Someone's serenading me! *(She darts to balcony curtains, peers out)* What I see! Your daughter's talking to a stranger. That's indiscreet of her. He's very handsome. She should turn him over to me. Pedro's not jealous of me. *(Trots back and kneels)* I shall speak to her. I shall reprimand her.

CAPUCHO

There are a lot of strangers in town—very noisy—very noisy—

INES

Well, rhubarb-stalk, why don't you roll? (CAPUCHO *rolls*) Ah, Cobra's peepers—you are not in the vein, my pumpkin seed—you are not in the vein. (CAPUCHO *goes to the window, peers out.* INES *picks up the dice, shakes them elaborately*) You're too tense, my peanut. Play casually. (*She exchanges dice*) When I play I think of something else. How I will look at Easter. Won't I be beautiful?

CAPUCHO

(*Returning from window*)

Are we playing or talking? Play! (INES *throws dice.*)

INES

Two hundred pesos—little dice, buy me this robe my heart longs for. (*She peers at them*) Ah! Six! (CAPUCHO *starts to pick up the dice for her*) I'll pick them up! (*She rolls again*) Ah! Four and two. (CAPUCHO *wants to kill her*) You see, Capucho. I don't even think about it. Well, that's all. Pay up, dried apricot. My robe, my beautiful robe is paid for.

CAPUCHO

One more.

INES

To increase your losses? No—you shouldn't play this game. It's not your metièr. Pay up!

CAPUCHO

You've got to give me a chance to win back.

INES

Two hundred pesos. Forty I have—a hundred and eighty you owe me. With the rest I will buy you something.

CAPUCHO

Don't buy me anything—it will cost me too much.

INES

Shall I get you earrings like the sailors wear? You'll look like a kippered tar that's had fifty years of service. Or would you prefer a tattoo? I'll stand you a tattoo. (CAPUCHO, *ready to roll, picks up dice, weighs them, realizes they are loaded.*)

CAPUCHO

Loaded! You cheat your own husband!

INES

I have no prejudices. Let it be a lesson to you. (*The noise of the tumult in the square comes in through the window*) What a noise outside! What a tumult! (*She runs again to the window*) Those men have taken possession of the whole square. (MANUELA *has come in with* LIZARDA. *She is very warm. She starts at once the process of disrobing, taking one garment off after another. Then with* LIZARDA's *help she puts on a negligee which she has on by the time* SERAFIN *enters.*)

95

MANUELA

(*In despair*)

How often do I have to beg you two to stay in your own apartments? Twenty rooms in this house and not an inch to myself.

CAPUCHO

(*Holding up the dice*)

Loaded!

INES

Ah—flirt—flirt—and in the public square too!

CAPUCHO

Loaded!

INES

To belabor the obvious, daughter, your father is a dunce.

MANUELA

And to think that when I woke this morning I was at peace.

INES

What troubles you, daughter? The tall stranger, perhaps? Ah, that is a sign of youth—that is a sign of vitality. When we're not troubled, we might as well be dead. I'm glad for you, daughter.

CAPUCHO

Loaded! I see it now, Manuela, she's been playing me with loaded dice for years. She's been cheating me for years.

MANUELA

Please, Father, go away, and take Mother with you.

INES

You request the minnow to remove the whale.

CAPUCHO

(*Wailing*)

My wife—my own wife!

INES

I'm standing him a tattoo. His chest is so narrow it won't take a panorama. It will have to be a miniature.

MANUELA

You drive me mad, both of you. (INES *goes to window.*)

INES

Oh! Oh! Look, Manuela! Oh! Oh! (SERAFIN *calmly steps into the room from the balcony. In one hand he carries* MANUELA's *parasol; his shoes in the other.* INES *retreats, then advances toward him with a little cry.* MANUELA *pales, stares at him.*)

SERAFIN

I sense in this room an atmosphere of strangulated discomfort. These must be relatives. Won't you introduce me?

MANUELA

Unfortunately, I do not know your name.

SERAFIN

Oh, yes, I think you do. I took the trouble to tell it to you My name is . . .

MANUELA
(*Doesn't want him to tell*)
Unfortunately it has escaped my mind. (*Introducing*) My mother and my father.

SERAFIN

How do you do?

INES

Have you an appointment?

SERAFIN

I happened to be in the neighborhood. I thought I'd drop in. She left her umbrella.

INES

You take a great deal of trouble to return an umbrella.

MANUELA

Oh, he gets about in the oddest way!

INES

He walked the rope. How interesting! There, filbert, is a man!

CAPUCHO
(*Offering dice*)

Roll?

SERAFIN

No, thank you. I never gamble before lunch.

INES

(*Flirting*)

Are you staying for lunch?

SERAFIN

(*Declining politely*)

Well, I don't know—perhaps . . .

INES

Manuela, invite him to lunch.

MANUELA

You don't have to invite him!

CAPUCHO

(*Happy*)

Then we'll roll after lunch. Won't you put on your shoes and stay?

SERAFIN

Thank you very much. I am not a gentleman of leisure. I . . .

INES

(*Following up*)

And after lunch we could go for a drive in the country by ourselves. Would you like that?

SERAFIN

I'm sorry.

MANUELA
(*Relieved*)

You see, Mother, he won't take yes for an answer.

INES

I'm not a hag, you know. My arms and shoulders are still beautiful.

SERAFIN

Manuela, have you always been subject to this sulphuric rivalry?

INES

Are you married?

SERAFIN
(*Looking straight at* MANUELA)

I am engaged.

INES

Fortunate girl!

SERAFIN

Thank you, mother-in-law.

MANUELA

What an imagination! Stops at nothing!

SERAFIN
(*To* INES)

I am a visionary like your daughter, only slightly more practical.

INES

I see the way things are blowing. (*To* MANUELA) Chicka-dee, are you sly? Remember on which side our bread is buttered! Don't trifle with my future!

MANUELA

Don't worry, Mother. Pedro will be home any minute. I imagine by then our guest will have departed to his—more important activities.

SERAFIN

(*Looking at her*)

Yes. But not alone.

INES

I'll be glad to go with you—anywhere.

SERAFIN

Thank you.

INES

Now, don't be tiresome. Stay for lunch. Pedro will adore you.

SERAFIN

I'm sure.

INES

We'll have a battle of wits. Epigrams will flow.

CAPUCHO

And an excellent wine.

INES

But we still don't know your name. We can't just say,
"This is a gentleman who came in through the window," can
we? What is your name?

MANUELA
(*To protect* SERAFIN)
He prefers to remain incognito.

INES
(*Delighted*)
Incognito! Have you done something? How wonderful!

SERAFIN

I am Estramudo the Pirate.

INES

Merciful Mother of God!

CAPUCHO
(*On the run*)
I'll fetch Pedro! (*He disappears.*)

SERAFIN

My time is limited. I have a performance to give. I'm
afraid you must leave us alone.

MANUELA

Don't leave us.

SERAFIN

(*Grabbing* MANUELA *by the wrists*)

There is a practical side to successful piracy that you do not visualize in your dreams. You might as well get used to it.

MANUELA

Mother, you must stay.

INES

(*Making for the door*)

He doesn't want me. (*She returns; she keeps making little runs between* SERAFIN *and the door*) The fact is, Reverend Pirate—my daughter's marriage was a business arrangement, contrived by me. It's time she had a little fling. Have a little fling, daughter. I'll watch for Pedro. It will ease my conscience. (*Toddles back again, to* SERAFIN) I'm sympathetic, aren't I? May I touch you? My other son-in-law adores me. (*She flutters out.*)

SERAFIN

(*Takes a step toward* MANUELA)

Well, Manuela, we meet again.

MANUELA

At least once too often.

SERAFIN

Don't trifle with me, madame. It is not lightly I have revealed my identity. All the jackals in the province will scent prey. If I have risked this much for another sight of you, do you think I will stop now?

MANUELA

Bandit! Murderer! If you come near me I'll scream.

SERAFIN

Why should you scream? I'm prepared to be charming to you. (*Takes up book which* MANUELA *has left on the bed*) Let's see what he has to say—my anonymous biographer.

MANUELA

You have misunderstood me. I was naive enough to talk to you as I would to—a friend. This is how you repay me— by rushing into my room like a robber baron. This is not the Middle Ages, you know. (*She makes an attempt to retrieve the book*) Give me my book.

SERAFIN

Inadequate. Totally inadequate.

MANUELA

I'll never forgive you for this arrogance.

SERAFIN

Does he think it's as easy as this—this scribbler? Doesn't he realize, this dilettante— (*He taps the book contemptuously*) doesn't he realize that piracy on the scale on which

I practice it is big business? It's a desk job! I assure you, Manuela, that from dawn to dusk and all through the night I slave in my cabin over graphs and meteorological tables and astrolabes. No exercise. As a result I suffer terribly from heartburn.

MANUELA

Every minute you remind me more of Pedro. Except that he is less conceited.

SERAFIN

(*Leafs through the book*)

Ah! The harem episode.

MANUELA

You escaped with nine wives, didn't you?

SERAFIN

Yes.

MANUELA

Were you happy—the ten of you?

SERAFIN

When you run away with nine women, it seldom lasts. (*Taps the book again*) What he doesn't seem to understand is that it was not I who escaped from the harem. I was very happy there—excellent food—a bit on the rich side—companionship—when I wanted it—I didn't escape—it was the women who escaped. . . .

105

MANUELA

(*Withering*)

Wanted to get you to themselves, of course?

SERAFIN

Partly. They spirited me away because they wanted my money, my horses and my knowledge of the terrain. . . .

MANUELA

Well, I'm glad that your sense of total irresistibility wavers for once. (SERAFIN *shuts the book and throws it on bed*) I shall never look at that book again. You've spoiled it for me.

SERAFIN

Poor Manuela, the actuality that surrounds you is so drab— your husband, these incredible parents—no wonder you seek escape. Well, I have set a task for myself. To convert you to the beauty and excitement of reality.

MANUELA

Personified in you!

SERAFIN

Yes. (*He looks at her a moment, then crosses to the door, locks it and puts the key in his pocket.*)

MANUELA

(*Terrified*)

What are you doing?

SERAFIN

Ensuring privacy.

MANUELA

Give me that key!

SERAFIN

Sorry.

MANUELA

(*Looks at him as if for the first time*)

So this is the Great Estramudo! Would-be lover who resorts to locked doors. Braggart. Complacent. Murders by graph. Drowns from a desk. Loots by logarithm. On what flimsy bases do reputations rest!

SERAFIN

You forget one thing . . .

MANUELA

If your task was to disillusion me, I can assure you you have succeeded. I shall pick up where I left off with Napoleon.

SERAFIN

(*Pensively*)

He gets heartburn. He's a sedentary fellow.

MANUELA

I hope he never drops in here. While he's safe at St. Helena I can dream about him. Heroes mustn't approach. You prove that.

SERAFIN

You forget I'm risking my life for you.

MANUELA

(*Regards him narrowly*)

Aren't you rather self-conscious about it?

SERAFIN

(*Bursting out in fury*)

Of course I'm self-conscious. Of whom else should I be conscious? I'm all I've got!

MANUELA

I shan't increase your holdings.

SERAFIN

You drive me crazy. You know that, don't you?

MANUELA

The solution is simple. A short walk, over that rope, to Isabella's.

SERAFIN

Isabella seems to be on your mind.

MANUELA

Yes, I'm insanely jealous, don't you see?

SERAFIN

(*Quietly*)

By scoffing at what you feel you will not diminish the irritation.

MANUELA

How happy you must be!

SERAFIN

(*Looks at her, calmly*)

Not yet, but I will be.

MANUELA

If you are this pirate, why have you penetrated your own disguise? Why have you confessed publicly to being the hunted Estramudo?

SERAFIN

To interest you!

MANUELA

You don't think you could do it on your own?

SERAFIN

I'm a modest man.

MANUELA

If I had read this in a book I should have thought: "How romantic! How noble." But as I see you, as I know you, I feel impatient that you should pay such a price—for a gesture!

SERAFIN

(*With a swift glance toward the bed*)

I had hoped, madame, for more than a gesture.

MANUELA

(*Inexorable*)

For a gesture!

SERAFIN

You have a penchant for romance. I played romantic.

MANUELA

It is all very well to play romantic, but in real life one wants common sense. You're stupid not to see that.

SERAFIN

I thought common sense bored you.

MANUELA

(*Wailing*)

Don't argue. Now that my mother knows who you are, it will be all over town in five minutes.

SERAFIN

Surely she wouldn't tell—a fatal secret like that.

MANUELA

Telling fatal secrets's the breath of her nostrils. I implore you. Go. Get away while you can.

SERAFIN
(Flatly)

No.

MANUELA
(Desperate)

You won't go?

SERAFIN
(Finally)

Won't go!

MANUELA
(Whispering)

Why—why?

SERAFIN

Because it would be the height of idiocy to have put myself into this jeopardy—for nothing!

MANUELA

I am touched by your recklessness.

SERAFIN

That's not enough.

MANUELA

But if you're captured and hanged . .

SERAFIN

The memory will suffice. But give me the memory.

III

MANUELA
(*Making a desperate last stand*)

No—no.

SERAFIN

Manuela—do not make me ridiculous—do not make me risk all—for nothing!

MANUELA

(*Another step backward, her desperation rising, a kind of last stand to bolster herself. He finally has her cornered*)
You don't know me.

SERAFIN

I quiver to make your acquaintance!

MANUELA

You said I was a dreamer. That is only one facet of my character.

SERAFIN

You are a glorious prism that dazzles me with all its facets. . . .

MANUELA

No. Listen. . . .

SERAFIN

I listen but I hear only the pounding of one voice.

MANUELA

(*She eludes him for a moment and rushes across the room. Desperately*)
I am a wife.

112

SERAFIN

You've mentioned that. That's not an argument, it's a condition.

MANUELA

I have kept my marriage going. That is an act of will. Less exciting perhaps than scuttling ships on the high seas, but requiring a steadiness and a tenacity of its own.

SERAFIN

But, Manuela, all this steadiness and tenacity must require strenuous effort. I want to make life easier for you. I want to substitute adventure and experience. Oh, Manuela, come with me, escape with me.

MANUELA

With a man I hardly know?

SERAFIN

I hardly know you either. We'll have the excitement of discovery. (*Dreaming aloud*) It will be heaven, Manuela.

MANUELA

If it's heaven you want, you'll get there quicker if you stay here.

SERAFIN

I want you to share my life. We'll begin by touring these enchanted islands—pitching our show in those little towns drowsing away in the valleys.

MANUELA

And I'll be queen of the gypsies, I suppose!

SERAFIN

Yes, and after a year or so of sensational obscurity—we shall make our debut in Madrid.

MANUELA

You mean you'll make your debut in Madrid. What will I be doing? Mending your socks? My dear friend, I am not the sort of person who can just step out of the house and start on a world tour without a hat.

SERAFIN

Take a hat.

MANUELA

Before even the slightest journey, even an imaginative one, I have to pack carefully.

SERAFIN

We would have a glorious life, Manuela. Already we have missed so many springs, so many summers. Shall we miss the rest?

MANUELA

I'm afraid we must.

SERAFIN

(*Following up*)

After all, it's a mere geographical accident that separated us.

MANUELA

It separates so many people.

SERAFIN

(*Pressing on*)

We might have grown up together.

MANUELA

Not for long. You would have run away to some other Manuela separated from you by geography.

SERAFIN

(*Coming closer*)

I cannot believe destiny would be so perverse—to give me the vision and then to snatch it away.

MANUELA

(*Realistically*)

Destiny is often perverse. It is even malicious. You live by your wits. I am a housewife. I love routine. I couldn't possibly live as you do.

SERAFIN

Can it be, Manuela, that you want me to settle down? Very well.

MANUELA

I can't imagine you settled down. Keep to the life you really love. We're not for each other.

SERAFIN

The lonely road again—the canopy of stars. Not tonight, Manuela. This canopy— (*Grabbing* MANUELA's *hands and holding her close*) less glittering, but more alluring.

MANUELA
(*Struggling*)

Let me go!

SERAFIN

Never while I live

MANUELA

I warn you—if you destroy what I have built up I shall despise you—I shall hate you.

SERAFIN

What you have built up is a lie. I must do violence to it because you haven't the strength to abandon it by yourself.

MANUELA

What do you know of my strength? How dare you make these large assumptions! How dare you estimate me on an hour's acquaintance? What makes you think I'm so naive? I don't really believe you're Estramudo— Let me go! Let me go!

PEDRO
(*From off stage. He has tried the door and found it locked*)
Manuela, let me in—let me in, I say—it's Pedro.

THE PIRATE

MANUELA

My husband!

SERAFIN

Good! Let's have this out once and for all. (*He strides to the door, unlocks it and admits* PEDRO. *Then returns to his argument with* MANUELA *as if they were alone in the room.* PEDRO *stands, watching them*) I'm prepared, even if you are not, to face the facts of your life. My imaginings are precise and practical, yours are nebulous.

MANUELA

Mine have not led me to violence and crime. (*They face each other. There is now a blazing antagonism between them.*)

SERAFIN

You and I have far to go, dear madame, before we understand each other.

MANUELA

However far we went we should never meet. We are those parallel lines which, the scientists tell us, though they reach into infinity, still may never meet.

SERAFIN

I refuse to submit our relationship to a law of physics.

MANUELA

That will not alter the law.

SERAFIN

They shall curve like light, these parallel lines, till we converge. (PEDRO *stands there, puffing, his eyes bulging, looking at his wife backed against the bed by the importunate* SERAFIN. *Neither moves a muscle—though they both know he is there. They are in each other's eyes.*)

PEDRO

(Can stand no more)

Do you two realize that I am in the room! (PEDRO *feels a mixture of anger and fear.* SERAFIN: *How much has he told* MANUELA? *Does she already know? At the same time his jealousy roils him. He wants to kill them both.*)

MANUELA

Pedro, this man is not here by my invitation. I beg you to believe that.

PEDRO

The guard at the door did not see him pass. You must have slipped him by. . . .

SERAFIN

(Bearing down on him)

For me walls are porous. You should know that if anybody does. (PEDRO *sweats.*)

PEDRO

I ought to kill you both.

SERAFIN

You'd miss us!

THE PIRATE

MANUELA

Pedro, husband, this man annoys me. Put him out.

SERAFIN

Yes, put me out, Pedro!

PEDRO

(Unable to bear it longer—to MANUELA*)*
What has he told you? What has he said to you?

SERAFIN

I have had the courage to tell her the truth!

PEDRO

The truth? What truth? (*He wipes his streaming forehead.*)

SERAFIN

Is it warm? You are sweating.

PEDRO

(Desperate to know)
What has he said to you?

MANUELA

He is full of tall tales intended to impress me with his
grandeur. They do not impress me. They weary me.

PEDRO

What's he told you?

MANUELA

That I may not tell you.

SERAFIN

(*Easily*)

Everyone in the village knows it by now. Why shouldn't
he?

PEDRO

(*To protect himself in case*)

Whatever he's told you is a lie—I tell you that, Manuela—
a gross lie.

SERAFIN

This is not a lie and he of all men knows it.

MANUELA

Why he of all men?

PEDRO

(*Sure now* SERAFIN *has revealed his identity*)

It's not true. He's a cheating mountebank—I'll have him
run out of town. . . . (*In his agitation he drops his rabbit's
foot. He starts to pick it up but* SERAFIN'S *voice is so searing
that he neglects to do it.*)

SERAFIN

Is it a lie that *I am* Estramudo the Pirate? You dropped
your rabbit's foot. I, Estramudo, as you, my sometime captor
—well know me.

PEDRO

What?

MANUELA

(*Her eyes lighting*)

He your captor?

SERAFIN

Even he.

MANUELA

(*Appealing to* PEDRO)

Pedro, what's he saying?

PEDRO

(*Sweating profusely*)

I don't know what he's talking about.

SERAFIN

(*Advances on him menacingly*)

Jog your brain, Pedro. Jog your brain. And please to remember that Estramudo has decimated cities merely because he disliked the food in the leading restaurant. Neither your rabbit's foot nor your misplaced relationship to this lady will give you sanctuary. Do not presume too far. Do not call Estramudo a liar!

PEDRO

(*Completely taken aback. Runs behind* MANUELA *as if for protection*)

You—you—what is this? What do you say?

MANUELA

Don't be frightened, Pedro. No matter what he says I don't believe him. He brags.

SERAFIN

But your husband knows that I speak the truth.

MANUELA

Nonsense, how would he know?

SERAFIN

But, dear Manuela, it's really one of the ironies of history.

MANUELA

Is it really?

SERAFIN

That Pedro there—bristling with amulets and barricaded by rabbits' feet—should be the one man alive who nearly did me in. The one man alive!

PEDRO

What!

MANUELA

Pedro!

SERAFIN

He captured me! The only man who ever succeeded in that —he captured me!

MANUELA

Pedro!

SERAFIN

Come back, Pedro. Tell her. Reconstruct the scene—you know, the burning deck of the *Excelsior*. He was returning from a business trip to Algiers. I attacked his ship—purely routine job—everything was going with monotonous smoothness when this Pedro—this very Pedro . . .

MANUELA

Well, what happened? What did he do?

SERAFIN

It never occurred to me—he was much slimmer in those days, I must say. . . .

MANUELA
(*To* PEDRO)

He does know you then?

PEDRO

We met.

MANUELA

You met!

SERAFIN

We certainly met. And he wasn't very polite about it either. He sneaked around me and manacled me from the rear.

MANUELA
(*Astonished*)

Pedro did!

123

SERAFIN

Pedro did. What was that voice, Pedro? That mysterious voice that frightened me so? What was that voice?

PEDRO·

No, no.

SERAFIN

Am I or am I not Estramudo the Pirate? Mene mene . . .

PEDRO

(*Very cunning, begins to see a way out for himself*)
Yes, he is Estramudo the Pirate.

SERAFIN

All your doubts vanished, madame?

MANUELA

(*Gazing at* PEDRO *with admiration*)
Yes, they are vanished.

SERAFIN

No more skepticism?

MANUELA

(*Still loking at* PEDRO)
No. Pedro! You captured him!

PEDRO

(*Gasping and wiping his forehead*)
Yes.

124

MANUELA

Why have you never told me? Why didn't you tell me?

PEDRO

(*Shuffling around*)

I don't know—I . . .

MANUELA

But why? Darling. Why?

PEDRO

It didn't seem worth mentioning.

MANUELA

It didn't seem worth mentioning!

SERAFIN

(*Very annoyed*)

Manuela, you seem to miss the point.

MANUELA

And what is the point?

SERAFIN

The point is not that your husband, by the merest fluke interrupted my operations, but that I am Estramudo and that I escaped and that my exploits ever since have been on a grander scale than ever.

MANUELA

On the contrary.

SERAFIN

On the contrary, what?

MANUELA

The point is that Pedro, unaided, captured you and never even mentioned it. The heroism of it—the modesty of it!

SERAFIN

Well, what do you want, a hero or a shrinking violet? I wish you'd make up your mind which.

MANUELA

Both—and it appears my husband is both. (*To* ESTRAMUDO) You said you would show me the beauty and excitement of reality—you have. I see them now—I see them in Pedro.

SERAFIN

You have a microscopic eye!

MANUELA

Did you hear what he just said? It didn't seem worth mentioning! And indeed he never mentioned it—he never told me. Often when I have reproached him for being stodgy, all he need have said was, "Well, I may be a stick-in-the-mud, but I captured Estramudo. I put Estramudo in irons." But he never said it. He never breathed it. Dear, magnificent, neglected, heroic Pedro—forgive me!

126

PEDRO

(*Relieved—cashing in; magnanimously*)

It's all right, Manuela!

MANUELA

(*Clinging to him*)

I'll make it up to you. I promise you, dearest, from now on I shall make it up to you.

PEDRO

(*Modestly*)

Forget it!

MANUELA

Never, I'll never forget it. (PEDRO *begins to preen a bit; he sees himself in a new role. He likes it.*)

PEDRO

As a matter of fact, Manuela, it took a lot of nerve!

MANUELA

Nerve he calls it! What it must have taken—nerve! I'm sure it did.

SERAFIN

Well, of all the incalculable, irrational women I have ever met, you, Manuela, take the cake.

MANUELA

(*Not taking her eyes from* PEDRO)

What did he say, dear?

SERAFIN

(*Events have taken a disastrous turn; at his wits' end*)

What will you do? Stay here and keep your spirit alive with the opiate of dreams, or will you come with me? Which shall it be?

PEDRO

How far do you think you'd get?

SERAFIN

Beyond your little vision, my good Pedro. I have engagements on the seven seas. Will you keep them with me?

MANUELA

I'm not a marine compass.

SERAFIN

I warn you if I go now it may be forever.

MANUELA

You transform eternity into a pleasant interlude.

SERAFIN

You risk farewell?

MANUELA

I encourage it.

SERAFIN

I had the illusion that you were the woman who could allay for me the hunger that gnaws at the heart of every man,

128

for he knows not what. That you could bridge for me the chasm between the infinite and the finite. (*Sits on stool and takes off shoes for the return journey*) I see now that it was an illusion. However, I bear you no malice. I hope you will both come to my performance this evening.

PEDRO

Surely you're not going on with that now.

SERAFIN

More than ever. My identity is being circulated through the village. As a result we'll sell out. You don't expect me to walk out on a sold-out house. It isn't natural. My livelihood may be piracy, but my avocation is art. (*He starts toward the window.*)

MANUELA
(*Involuntarily, scared*)
Don't do that again—take the stairs.

SERAFIN

Stairs bore me. I go by air. (*And he is off through the balcony outside the curtained French windows and presumably over his special highway. Instinctively,* MANUELA *runs to the window and watches the crossing.*)

MANUELA

Thank God!

PEDRO
What for? (*She stands watching, strained in every nerve.*

PEDRO *is eyeing her like a hawk*) Did he make it? (*She doesn't answer. She can't speak.* PEDRO *resumes, with a kind of vindictive caginess*) Oh, you're relieved, I see. You seem to have changed sides all of a sudden. Or were you always on his?

MANUELA
(*Sinks to a chair*)
Why are you so bitter?

PEDRO
Because you're a wanton. Do you think because I'm fat I'm blind?

MANUELA
(*Looks at him, pleading*)
Pedro . . .

PEDRO
This hero—this Estramudo—this lover of your dreams . . .

MANUELA
Pedro, I beg you. . . .

PEDRO
(*Slyly*)
And yet—dashing as he is, I captured him. I put him in irons. I nearly did him in. And, as you say, I never spoke of it. Kept it to myself. Modest, wasn't it?

MANUELA
I wish you would allow your virtues to be discovered instead of ramming them down my throat!

130

THE PIRATE

PEDRO

(Same sly manner)

Coincidence, isn't it?

MANUELA

What? (*She is frightened by the manifest cruelty in his tone and manner, his air of a cat playing with a mouse.*)

PEDRO

Well, you dream of this man—you read books about him —and then he appears—in the flesh, you might say. He appears—quite a coincidence—a miracle, you might say.

MANUELA

(Gets up, unable to bear more. She looks at him. His mood is beyond her, sinister)

I don't like you in this cat and mouse vein, Pedro. What are you thinking?

PEDRO

You know, Manuela, I'm beginning to think—now you probably won't agree with me—but I'm beginning to think I'm not considerate enough—as a husband, I mean.

MANUELA

Now you really worry me!

PEDRO

I mean it. For instance, we never go on trips together. You're always talking about how you like to travel and yet we never do. That's wrong. That's very wrong. We shall alter that. I'm going to take you on a trip. Wherever you'd like to go—within reason. What do you say?

MANUELA

(*Sits on bed*)

This is so sudden, Pedro. (PEDRO *has sidled to the balcony windows, peeps out through the curtains.*)

PEDRO

He's out there in the square, your lover, putting up his show-tent. Cool, I'll say that for him—cool!

MANUELA

(*Trying to sound casual, fighting for time*)

He's my lover now, is he? Lucky for you I haven't quite got your tempo.

PEDRO

Do you deny that you are attracted by him?

MANUELA

No.

PEDRO

You don't deny it!

MANUELA

I never have denied it.

PEDRO

You love this Estramudo.

132

THE PIRATE

MANUELA

This seems to be an obsession of yours.

PEDRO

You fool! You blind, deluded fool! If you knew! If you only knew! The gods themselves are laughing at you. If you knew!

MANUELA

You keep saying, if I knew—if I knew what?

PEDRO

This Estramudo—you let him be your lover. Don't deny it. (*In a sudden rage he slaps her face*) I know it's true.

MANUELA

(*Flaring up, to wound him*)
I don't deny it. It is my only pride—my only joy.

PEDRO

(*His fists clench, his veins stand out on his forehead*)
Estramudo. You love Estramudo! (*His voice rises shrilly*)
Very glamorous—in the book. Very romantic—in the book. The harem episode. Very entertaining—oh, yes—in the book. But do you want to know what really happened? He didn't elope with those nine women. Oh, no! The Sultan asked him to get rid of them because they were getting on his nerves and Estramudo took them out and drowned them—every one. He got paid for it. He did it on commission. This is your Estramudo!

MANUELA

(*Quietly*)

How do you know all this?

PEDRO

The Sultan was a customer of mine—that's how I know it! I sold him cannonballs. He told me. This is the man you dream about. This is the man you idealize.

MANUELA

I don't believe it. I don't believe he could do such things.

PEDRO

He could and he has. And more—truly unbelievable things —nameless things. If you knew—if you imagined—you wouldn't adore him quite so much, this Estramudo!

MANUELA

If all you say is true, then he's not—I'm sure he's not Estramudo.

PEDRO

He's admitted it, hasn't he? He's said so, hasn't he? I captured him, didn't I?

MANUELA

(*Beginning to be overcome by the growing incongruities*)

I don't know, Pedro. This is all very strange.

PEDRO

I'll prove to you that he is Estramudo. I'll prove it.

MANUELA

How?

PEDRO

You heard him say I manacled him. How do you think he got away after that? I am a firm believer, you know, in the profit system. I made a bargain with him. I made him turn over to me the loot he'd gathered in twenty years of successful practice. That was my price for letting him off.

MANUELA

You still have this loot?

PEDRO

Part of it.

MANUELA

Oh—gave most of it to charity, I suppose?

PEDRO

(*Piously*)

You know I do many good works.

MANUELA

(*Feels herself on the trail of something*)

Have you any of it left?

135

PEDRO

Hidden beneath the floor of the barn at our summer place I have some of the choicest pieces. They'd make your mouth water.

MANUELA
(*Half to herself*)

Fantastic.

PEDRO
(*Sits beside her on the bed*)

Fantastic indeed. Buried there I have the diamond necklace of Marie Antoinette, the emerald and ruby stomacher of the Great Catherine . . .

MANUELA

What are you going to do with that? You can't wear it, can you?

PEDRO

It's a nice thing to have.

MANUELA

You have these things beneath the floor of our barn?

PEDRO
(*Not wanting to be too specific*)

Oh, well, some of them. Do you believe it now—that he is Estramudo? (*He gets up, starts for the balcony again*) Well, in any case he has admitted it. For that alone he will hang.

136

MANUELA
(*Rises*)

Pedro, I'm willing to promise never to see him again.

PEDRO

Yes, you will—at least once. I promise you that—at least
once. A very imposing occasion. (*He suddenly bursts into an
uncontrollable laugh.* MANUELA *looks at him, studies him.
She is seized with a cold fear. His mirth frightens her.*)

MANUELA
(*Finally*)

You find things funny?

PEDRO

Very.

MANUELA

Would it be too much to ask you to share the joke with
me?

PEDRO

You wouldn't enjoy it. No, you wouldn't. (*His laughter
simmers down, but not his gaiety. He executes a dance step.*)

MANUELA

You are so happy you dance!

PEDRO
(*Stops the step*)

Oh, no!

137

MANUELA

Feeling awfully well, aren't you?

PEDRO

Not bad.

MANUELA

Why are you in such good spirits?

PEDRO

(*Canny and secretive again*)

I'm not particularly. (*He sings.*)

MANUELA

You sing, you dance.

PEDRO

(*Same voice*)

That's odd!

MANUELA

It is indeed. You seldom sing, Pedro, and you rarely dance.

PEDRO

Quite true. Well, I must be off.

MANUELA

Where are you going?

PEDRO

(*Casually*)

To the Capitol.

MANUELA

The Capitol! Why?

PEDRO

A little business at the Capitol.

MANUELA

Your business at the Capitol would not by any chance include a visit to the Viceroy, would it, Pedro?

PEDRO

How keen you are, my dear! How intuitive! I may look in on the Viceroy. I may. (*Looks out the window*) Think of it, Manuela. To see your lover mixed up in all that tomfoolery out there you wouldn't think there was a price on his head. And what a price—hundred thousand pesos. Round sum—global!

MANUELA

Please don't do this, Pedro. In all the years I've been your wife I've never begged anything of you. I beg you now—don't inform on him. Look, I'm prepared to see you in a new light. I've promised never to see him again. I'll devote myself to you.

PEDRO

But your devotion is my right. You promised it at the altar. So you see I'll have it anyway!

MANUELA

What makes you so sure?

THE PIRATE

PEDRO

It is your eccentricity to be honest.

MANUELA

To you honesty is merely a weakness to be exploited.

PEDRO

Something in what you say. Well, good-bye, my dear. Oh
—first a slight precaution: to cut your friend's arterial highway. (*He takes out knife, goes to balcony. He disappears on
balcony with knife.* MANUELA *notices* PEDRO'S *rabbit's foot,
picks it up, finds it contains a charm, takes it out. She looks
at the charm, reads the inscription, exclaims, replaces charm,
walks to bed and sits clutching rabbit's foot.*)

MANUELA

Pedro!

PEDRO
(*From balcony off stage*)

Well, there'll be no more rope walking! Put on something
handsome for tonight, Manuela. (*He returns from the balcony*) I shall take a box.

MANUELA
(*Handing him the rabbit's foot*)

Your rabbit's foot.

PEDRO
(*Startled, frightened*)

Where did you get that?

MANUELA

You dropped it.

PEDRO
(*Grabs it, pretends to be casual*)
Would have been bad luck to go to the Capitol without it.
Well, good-bye. (SERAFIN *comes in through the door, trembling with anger and carrying a rope.*)

SERAFIN
(*At white heat—to* PEDRO)
How dare you!

MANUELA

I thought stairs bored you.

SERAFIN
(*His eyes fixed on* PEDRO)
How dare you cut that rope!

MANUELA

It's his house.

SERAFIN
(*Without looking at her*)
It's my rope. I had my whole show hung on it and it
nearly fell into the square. You gave me a license, didn't you?
How dare you sabotage my performance?

MANUELA
It's not your performance, it's your approach.

141

SERAFIN

(*For the first time addressing her*)

You have shown where your sympathies lie, madame. That episode is over. (*Goes out on balcony to fix the rope.*)

PEDRO

Don't start that all over again. I'm off to the Capitol.

SERAFIN

(*Coming back in from balcony*)

The Capitol! Oh, are you? Will you do an errand for me there? Will you see the local manager for me and book our next engagement?

PEDRO

I'll be glad to. I'll get you a definite engagement!

SERAFIN

You're very kind. After the performance I hope I'll be in a position to buy you a drink.

MANUELA

(*Sits. Probing, to* SERAFIN)

If you're the great Estramudo, why are you so poor?

SERAFIN

It's my expensive Robin Hood reputation. I give everything to charity.

MANUELA

You too! Really, I hardly know which is which.

142

THE PIRATE

SERAFIN

(Puts an arm around PEDRO's *shoulder)*
We have so much in common, Pedro.

MANUELA

Not me!

SERAFIN

Certainly not you. *(To* PEDRO*)* It will be so much fun talking over old times.

PEDRO

We've got nothing to talk about.

SERAFIN

Oh, yes we have—the burning deck of the *Excelsior* . . .

MANUELA

(Still questioning)
When you gave him the Great Catherine's stomacher . . . ?

SERAFIN

I beg your pardon?

MANUELA

You gave him Catherine's stomacher, didn't you?

SERAFIN

I never met the lady, but if she had presented me with her stomacher, I shouldn't have given it to Pedro. I'd have put it in my memory book. I'd have saved it for you.

143

MANUELA

Thank you so much.

PEDRO

Well, I've got to be off. Good-bye.

SERAFIN
(With a bow to MANUELA*)*

Good-bye again, madame. Our relation is a perpetual fare-well.

PEDRO
(Very expansive. To SERAFIN*)*

Oh, you don't have to go.

SERAFIN
(Amazed)

Really?

PEDRO

Not at all. Why should you go? Stay. Make yourself at home.

SERAFIN

If you're so hospitable, why did you cut the rope?

PEDRO

Didn't want you to come in that way. Conspicuous. Neighbors gossip. As long as you come in respectably, through the front door, you're more than welcome. Good-bye, my dear one.

MANUELA

Don't go, Pedro! I warn you.

PEDRO

Sorry, my dear. (*To* SERAFIN) Farewell—Prince of Pirates. (*He goes.*)

SERAFIN

(*Looks after him—hands on hips*)

Irresistible, isn't he? Well, how do you account for this sudden cataract of courtesy?

MANUELA

You fool! Don't you see he's gone to the viceroy to inform on you? He's using me as a decoy to keep you here.

SERAFIN

So that's his game, is it? Well, what difference how long I live if only in the time I have left I know you love me. If only I die with that certitude. Say it, Manuela. Say it. Say you love me.

MANUELA

Oh, I do not deny I am attracted by you. I do not deny this stirring of love I feel for you.

SERAFIN

Then I have not wished through the years for an answering love for nothing. I knew it when I saw you in the square below. Shall I leave you now, when after all these years I have found you?

MANUELA

You face death!

SERAFIN

My beloved, do we not all?

MANUELA

While there is yet time, I beg you.

SERAFIN

And if we are parted, is that not another sort of death?

MANUELA

Our thoughts could wing the seas and touch.

SERAFIN

For so long I have been without the sight of your face, beyond the sound of your voice.

MANUELA

We could imagine another meeting in some happier future.

SERAFIN

You do love me then—you do feel then what I feel . . .

MANUELA

I want you to be alive. I want to look up at the sky and know that it covers you too.

146

SERAFIN

I long for a more intimate coverlet.

MANUELA

Don't joke.

SERAFIN

I'm not joking. For years I have lived on improvisation. The sight of you has sickened me of those bogus pearls strung on nothing. Emotionally, too, I have been on the dole. Oh, Manuela, up to today I've thought I lived in freedom. I see now it was loneliness.

MANUELA

Is this eloquence? Are these words?

SERAFIN

What does the voice tell you, the uncontaminated voice that whispers when freed from the bitter odds life jackets on us?

MANUELA

Must I watch you die?

SERAFIN

When that remote event occurs, I hope that you will be there. I should hate to outlive you, Manuela.

MANUELA

I'll do what I can to keep us contemporary— (*Suddenly thinking*) Tell me something.

147

SERAFIN

My heart's deepest secret.

MANUELA

Keep that for a minute. . . . Did you bribe Pedro with all your jewels?

SERAFIN

I beg your pardon?

MANUELA

Never mind—you'll have to excuse me—I must go now. (*Calling*) Lizarda.

SERAFIN

(*Enraged*)

What are you doing? I'm here by your husband's invitation. You can't do this to me! (LIZARDA *enters.*)

MANUELA

Lizarda, bring me my cloak and order the carriage. I'm going to our summer place.

LIZARDA

Yes, mistress. (*She goes out.*)

SERAFIN

(*Furious*)

I am risking my life for you, and you go riding in the country!

MANUELA

I am doing what I can to lessen that risk, do you mind?

SERAFIN

I will not have my sacrifice tampered with, do you hear! When I am on the way to the scaffold for the woman I love, I will not be tripped up, do you hear! I have done everything I can to jolt you out of this half-life you are living in, and you won't budge. You're immovable. I thought you were imaginative, you're not—you're stupid and conventional!

MANUELA

Are you quite finished?

SERAFIN

Yes, I'm finished.

MANUELA

Now you listen to me. You have the manners of a spoiled brat, and the effrontery of an unbridled egotist. Because I succumbed to your charm in the beginning, don't think I'll endure your temperament, because I won't!

SERAFIN

I'll never die for you again—never! (*He starts toward the window.*)

MANUELA

And don't make for that window. You go down those perfectly good stairs. (*Her tone is so imperious that it stops him;*

he has met his master; he turns and starts slowly for the door) And walk down too—don't use the bannister. (*He goes out like a whipped puppy.*)

MANUELA
(*The moment he is gone*)
The fool—the fool! (*Crosses to the window*) The romantic fool! (LIZARDA *enters, carrying* MANUELA's *cloak, she crosses to* MANUELA, *covers her with the cloak.*)

LIZARDA
(*Sighs*)
Oh, mistress. He's excessive overwhelmin'.

MANUELA
I'll try to save him. But if I fail—I'll never forgive him! (*She goes out.*)

Curtain

ACT THREE

ACT THREE

SCENE: *Early evening.* SERAFIN'S *show tent is now up, almost filling the stage between the two rows of houses. A miniature, coroneted proscenium, with green and white striped curtains, and in front of it the platform with its row of old-fashioned footlights. From the platform a runway, such as has been used in contemporary musical comedies. This runs forward almost to the actual footlights and the stage audience, when it comes in, sits on either side of it. The porches of* MANUELA'S *and* ISABELLA'S *houses form boxes.* SERAFIN *has draped the little iron railings of the porches so that they look quite gala.*

TRILLO, *greatly agitated, is hectically arranging* SERAFIN'S *props and costumes. Music comes from the town and from the hills; the rather weird punctuation of flamenco singing.* BOLO *comes in. He is also in considerable of a stir.*

TRILLO
(*Agitatedly*)
Well, Bolo, have you had any results with him?

BOLO
He won't go. Nothin' on earth can get him to go.

TRILLO
What's he doing?

BOLO

Acceptin' drinks from the gentry, disregardless of his peril. Tellin' stories of his piratical experiences. Actin' as if he wasn't practically hung already.

TRILLO

Fate has crept up on us. Listen to that singing. . . . He's got the whole town singing—music for his own hanging.

BOLO

I've half a mind to run away before the show. I advise you to get a move on too because it could be established you's a accomplice. What made him twine himself in this perilous complication?

TRILLO
(*Significantly*)

Sachet la femme.

BOLO

Riskin' his life for a woman! Can't you do anything with him, Trillo? He loves you. Can't you dissuade him?

TRILLO

He disregards me. All he says is—get ready the props—get ready the props. The curtain of the future is black, Bolo.

BOLO

I'm going to make a gi'antic effort. I'm going to threaten him. I'll abscond if he don't get away. If necessary, I'll resort to kidnapin'. (*A half-dozen soldiers enter; black-skinned and black-bearded, with scarlet uniforms and towering, tufted busbies.*)

TRILLO

The end is nigh! (OFFICER *enters.*)

OFFICER

Strict orders from the Viceroy. No member of the troupe is to leave the premises. (*He goes out.*)

BOLO

Too late long ago! (*Goes into tent.* LIZARDA *appears on* MAN-UELA's *balcony. She has a note in a sealed envelope in her hand. She whistles to* TRILLO.)

TRILLO

(*Looking up adoringly at* LIZARDA *on her balcony*)
That you, blissful?

LIZARDA

Blissful is just what I'm not. I'm overflowin' with apprehension.

TRILLO

It is true the night is fraught with peril.

LIZARDA

Fly! He must fly!

TRILLO

He won't fly.

LIZARDA

Then you must fly.

TRILLO

(*Stoutly*)

Where he is, there I is!

LIZARDA

My mistress has written a note to your mighty master. The fishnet of the law is noosin' you. The Viceroy's comin' to apprehend your master.

TRILLO

The Viceroy!

LIZARDA

Yes.

TRILLO

Himself?

LIZARDA

Himself.

TRILLO

That is formidable. That is sure . . .

LIZARDA

I pray you—my lady prays you . . .

TRILLO

Of old I know him. He will not take cover. . . .

LIZARDA

Then you both incurs the tight courtship of the law.

156

TRILLO

(*Stolidly*)

We courts it. (LIZARDA *sighs.* TRILLO *sighs. They look at each other*) Blissful—what is your other name?

LIZARDA

Lizarda.

TRILLO

Lizarda!

LIZARDA

And yours?

TRILLO

Trillo.

LIZARDA

Trillo. Oh, Trillo!

TRILLO

It was a case with me when first I beheld your sweet face, when first I heard your limpid voice—it was a case of a instantaneous conflagration! Whisper it, sweet Lizarda, what was the case with you?

LIZARDA

(*Breathing it out to the night*)

I was incinerated!

TRILLO

Is it not ironical that on this here night . . . ?

LIZARDA

On this here beloved night . . .

THE PIRATE

TRILLO

That on this here beloved night when we faces consummation we also faces grave peril . . .

LIZARDA

It is most malignant. Your mighty master—will he not fly?

TRILLO

Sweet cherub, do you not prognosticate? My master, he too, is struck with the rapture; he, too, is pierced with the dart.

LIZARDA

For my lady?

TRILLO

For your lady. Never have I known him so all-gone pierced. Through these long years of wear and tear I have observed him, sweet Lizarda, and this is the first time—the first time, I promise you, I have seen him clean transfixed. Therefore, lovely mistress, he will not fly.

LIZARDA

Perhaps this note—written in the fair hand of my lady . . .

TRILLO

Waft it to me, sweet Lizarda, and I will place it in his hand. (*She flutters down the note to him. He catches it.* ISA-BELLA *appears on her balcony and sees it.*)

ISABELLA

That note for me?

TRILLO

No, Mistress Galvez.

ISABELLA

If it's for your master, why not give it to me? I'm seeing him later and I'll deliver it.

LIZARDA
(To TRILLO*)*

No—no . . .

TRILLO
(To LIZARDA*)*

Never fear. (*To* ISABELLA) I can't do that, Mistress Galvez, 'cause this note is pressin'.

ISABELLA

I can imagine. What does it say?

TRILLO

Madam, it is my good fortune I can't read. (TRILLO *goes out.*)

ISABELLA
(To LIZARDA*)*

Lizarda, what's your mistress doing?

LIZARDA
(Crying)

Oh, Mistress Galvez, she is full of agitation.

159

ISABELLA

Really! How interesting! What about?

LIZARDA

I don't know, Mistress.

ISABELLA

Ask her to come out.

LIZARDA

She asked me not to disturb her, Mistress Galvez.

ISABELLA

Oh, nonsense. Tell her to come out and talk to me. I'll cheer her up. (PEDRO *comes in through the square. His clothes are dusty. He has ridden hard. He sees* ISABELLA *talking to* LIZARDA.)

PEDRO

Lizarda! Have I not forbidden you to talk to her?

LIZARDA

(*Frightened*)

Oh, Master. (PEDRO *turns to* ISABELLA.)

PEDRO

(*To* ISABELLA)

One of these days I'll have you flogged publicly.

ISABELLA

What fun for you!

PEDRO

(*To* LIZARDA)

What's your mistress doing?

LIZARDA

She's lying down, Master.

PEDRO

Tell her to get up. Tell her to get up and get dressed. Tell her she must look her best tonight. We're going to the show!

LIZARDA

Yes, Master.

PEDRO

At once—do you hear?

LIZARDA

Yes, Master.

PEDRO

Be quick about it.

LIZARDA

I'll tell her, Master. (*She goes inside.*)

ISABELLA

Well, Pedro, how do you like our new friend?

PEDRO
(*Expansive*)
Oh, I adore him. I'm very grateful to him!

ISABELLA
Generous husband!

PEDRO
Why not? Live and let live.

ISABELLA
(*Trying to wound him*)
He gets about, doesn't he?

PEDRO
He certainly gets about.

ISABELLA
Why don't you learn to walk the rope, Pedro?

PEDRO
Maybe I will!

ISABELLA
What are you so cheerful about anyway? (*A drum roll is heard and a bugle*) What's that?

PEDRO
(*In ecstasy*)
The bugle-call of the Viceroy's guard!

ISABELLA

Both of them?

PEDRO

He's here—the Viceroy's here.

ISABELLA

Will he be at the performance?

PEDRO

As my guest.

ISABELLA

Introduce me to him. If things go right I'll move to the Capitol.

PEDRO

You're far too ambitious, Madame Galvez.

ISABELLA

(*Snapping back*)

No more ambitious than your wife. I told you that mentally she takes excursions. This would seem to be a world tour! (*She disappears inside.*)

PEDRO

(*To himself, gloating*)

They're here—they're here! (*He executes a little dance step. As he reaches his doorstep a file of soldiers marches in. The soldiers take their places in double rank, facing the show-booth. PEDRO stands a minute, staring at them. His revenge is sweet*) My cup is full to running over! Let it run— Let it spill! (*He goes inside. The stage is deserted for a moment.* TRILLO *comes back.* SERAFIN *enters through the square.*)

TRILLO

Oh, Captain, I'm sure glad you got here!

SERAFIN
(*With a look at the soldiers*)
If the army wants to see the show, let them in for half price.

TRILLO

I have a note for you, Captain, from your lady. (SERAFIN *takes the note, reads it, puts it in his pocket*) Oh, Captain, I'm scared.

SERAFIN

Scared, Trillo? On the eve of triumph, scared? On the eve of recognition, scared?

TRILLO

Yes, Captain, plain scared.

SERAFIN

You didn't get out the props I wanted. Where's the revolving mirror?

TRILLO
(*Suspicious*)
What do you want with that?

164

SERAFIN

Never mind. Where is it?

TRILLO

Here it is. (TRILLO *gets long box, gives it to* SERAFIN.)

SERAFIN

Is it wound? Is it oiled? Is it true?

TRILLO

Yes, Captain, it's everything. (*Perturbed*) I hope you're not going to use that tonight, Captain. There's enough against us now.

SERAFIN
(*Over-riding him*)

And I want the crystal and the moonstone and the ebony funnel.

TRILLO
(*Very apprehensive*)

What are you up to, Captain?

SERAFIN
(*Casually*)

You will discover.

TRILLO

Captain, please don't employ these devices tonight.

SERAFIN

Why not?

TRILLO

The man you persuaded to concentrate on that mirror in
Valencia ain't waked up yet.

SERAFIN

That was a mistake. I had the misfortune to practice on a
victim of chronic sleeping-sickness.

TRILLO

I pray you, Captain, let us fly while there is yet time.

SERAFIN

·There is no time. Our backs are to the wall. Ingenuity,
not flight, will save us.

TRILLO

But the Viceroy's coming. (SERAFIN *sits on the stool and
starts to make up before a little mirror.*)

SERAFIN

We shall do our best to entertain him. I have played before
the King of Spain. I have appeared before the Khedive of
Egypt. Do you expect me to be cowed by the presence of a
provincial governor?

TRILLO

He ain't comin' because he's stage-struck.

SERAFIN

Why then?

166

TRILLO

Because it's broached his ears you're Estramudo and he wants the high honor to arrest you personal.

SERAFIN

We shall cope with the Viceroy.

TRILLO

What benefit from your copin' if you swing for it? (*Suddenly* DON BOLO, *wide-eyed with terror, sticks his head through the flaps of the door.*)

DON BOLO

The Viceroy!

TRILLO

(*Terrified, pleads*)

Please, Captain, let's amble.

SERAFIN

(*At his most commanding*)

Bolo, go out there. Greet the Viceroy in my behalf. Tell him we shall be pleased to receive him here. Do as I tell you, Bolo.

TRILLO

(*As he goes out with* BOLO)

We, who is about to die, salutes you. (*Music swells; soldiers enter and the* VICEROY. *He is an old man but erect and clearskinned; he is shrewd, sardonic and distinguished.* SERAFIN *advances to him, drops on one knee before him.*)

THE PIRATE

SERAFIN

I am honored, Excellency, that you have come this distance to see our little entertainment. I trust that our poor talents will yield not too scanty a reward for the ardors of your journey. We shall do our best.

VICEROY

(*Amused at* SERAFIN's *assumption that he has come to see the show*)

Do you imagine that my visit to you is esthetic?

SERAFIN

Our entertainment is not highbrow. A few songs, dancing, feats of magic, a little science.

VICEROY

Science also?

SERAFIN

I am a pupil of the great Mesmer. I have delved into the mysteries of animal magnetism. I perform experiments which may divert you.

VICEROY

You make me regret, alas, that I shall have to miss your entertainment.

SERAFIN
(*Innocent*)

Miss it, Excellency?

VICEROY

Unfortunately, I am afraid that you will have to miss it also. It is my unpleasant duty to arrest you.

SERAFIN

On what ground, Excellency?

VICEROY

For the moment it suits you to be an impresario. But it comes to my ears that you have an avocation somewhat more destructive.

SERAFIN

Will you arrest me, Excellency, on a rumor?

VICEROY

I arrest you on rumor. We shall try you on evidence. (*He nods to his men.*)

SERAFIN

(*Protesting*)

Excellency! (*Two* LIEUTENANTS *step forward and handcuff* SERAFIN *and then step back.*)

VICEROY

I am very sorry to have to do this. Our county jail is not too uncomfortable. I shall come to see you. As it happens, I knew Mesmer. His science fascinates me also. However, I hope you will not attempt to hypnotize the jailers. We shall have to put on guards who are complete extroverts. Good evening. (*The* VICEROY *turns to go.* SERAFIN *makes another circling movement. The two* LIEUTENANTS *go up the steps and stand in front of the two upstage exits left and right.*)

SERAFIN

One word, Excellency.

VICEROY
(*Turns*)

Well?

SERAFIN

I pray you, let me give this performance tonight . . .

VICEROY

What a passion for exhibitionism!

SERAFIN

Let me give this show, then do with me what you will.

VICEROY

You are a clever man. You must see that the procedure would be irregular.

SERAFIN

Put your men in the wings, but let me give the show.

VICEROY

If you escaped, I should have to consider myself a fool. I do not care to undervalue myself.

170

SERAFIN

It is not to escape. What chance to escape—with you here—with your men here?

VICEROY

Then why? Why?

SERAFIN

You are an imaginative man. You are a subtle man . . .

VICEROY

I cannot, in all honesty, contradict you. Still—there is a noose about your neck. Why?

SERAFIN

To answer that question—I shall have to give you a glimpse into my personal life. Do you mind?

VICEROY

(*Ironic, but interested*)

The vista fascinates me!

SERAFIN

I am in love, Excellency.

VICEROY

You have leisure for that also? What a crowded life!

SERAFIN

Love insinuates itself into the busiest of careers. Excellency, read this note. (*He hands him* MANUELA's *note. The* VICEROY *takes it, unfolds it and reads it, while* SERAFIN *hangs on him*) What do you think, Excellency? Is it encouraging? What is your opinion?

VICEROY

It is—enigmatic.

SERAFIN

(*Pouncing on the interpretation*)

That's just it, Excellency! How clever of you to have divined from that brief note her essential quality. Enigmatic! Compared to her, the Sphinx was a gossip writer.

VICEROY

(*Rather flattered*)

She is married?

SERAFIN

Oh, very.

VICEROY

They always are!

SERAFIN

Excellency, I know it is not your function to give advice to the lovelorn, but you are humane, you are human. Tell me what to do?

VICEROY

What have you to offer this lady?

SERAFIN

The future.

THE PIRATE

VICEROY

It threatens to be brief!

SERAFIN

What of that? Who said—"Life gives us but moments, and for those moments we give our lives"?

VICEROY

I'm afraid I don't understand that sort of thing.

SERAFIN

Were you never in love, Excellency?

VICEROY

(*Trying to remember*)

I suppose I must have been. . . . Let me see . . .

SERAFIN

Have you never wanted to die for a woman?

VICEROY

No! Yes—once—yes.

SERAFIN

(*In triumph*)

Ah!

VICEROY

Fortunately, I did not succeed.

173

THE PIRATE

SERAFIN

I hope I fail also. (*He is circling about the* VICEROY.)

VICEROY

Would you mind standing still? You make me dizzy.

SERAFIN

These are dizzy heights. I am on the brink of love. I am on the brink of death.

VICEROY

One thing I do not understand. If I let you give this show —what good will it do you?

SERAFIN

I want to hear her say it once. . . .

VICEROY

What?

SERAFIN

I want to hear her say, "I love you."

VICEROY

And if she does say it, will it not make this world more difficult to leave?

SERAFIN

On the contrary it will make the journey to the other bearable.

174

VICEROY

(*Laughs*)

Incomprehensible. (*Taps the note which he still has*) But the writer of this note does not wear her heart on her sleeve. How will you make her say she loves you?

SERAFIN

I don't know, Excellency.

VICEROY

You don't know!

SERAFIN

I live by improvisation.

VICEROY

I think you have a pretty shrewd idea. I'm curious, I must confess. . . . Still—I will be frank with you, my boy—would it surprise you to learn that I have a strong suspicon that you are not really Estramudo at all?

SERAFIN

Excellency, you must believe that!

VICEROY

However, if you insist you are Estramudo, I must take you at your word. But it is a dangerous game you are playing, my boy—more dangerous than you realize. You are a lover— in a world of cynics. You present me, for instance, with an

175

irresistible temptation. It is always helpful politically, you know, to capture an important criminal.

SERAFIN

I shall be only too happy, Excellency, to further your career.

VICEROY

(*Laughs*)

Now what does one do with a man like you?

SERAFIN

Put me in your memoirs.

VICEROY

I shall. With a chapter heading, "Help from an Unexpected Quarter." Well, you may give your show.

SERAFIN

Excellency!

VICEROY

When do you start?

SERAFIN

Whenever you're in the mood.

VICEROY

With your passion for acting, I wonder you bother with piracy.

176

SERAFIN

I am a lazy man, Excellency. Piracy is so much easier. Will you give us a few moments to make our preparations?

VICEROY

Very well. (*He hands the note to* SERAFIN *who reaches up and takes it with a free hand. The* VICEROY *turns to go, and suddenly wheels back as he realizes that* SERAFIN *has somehow gotten rid of the handcuffs*) Did I see correctly?

SERAFIN

(*Handing the handcuffs back to the* VICEROY)
I'm afraid you did. I could have returned these earlier but I didn't want you to feel insecure.

VICEROY
(*Grimly*)

My men will remain!

SERAFIN

Gladly.

VICEROY
(*As he hands the handcuffs to the* LIEUTENANT)
Don't take your eyes off him! (*To* SERAFIN) Tell me, did you really study with Mesmer or are you a congenital liar? Foolish question, don't bother to answer. (*To guards*) Stand back, men, give the impresario a little room. (*To* SERAFIN)

There's something rather perverse about this. I shall feel like a Roman Emperor of the decadence. Rather agreeable. (*He rings the bell of* PEDRO's *house*) Good luck tonight. I do wish I could have permitted you to remain. You might have had quite a run here—I shall miss you.

SERAFIN

It will be a pleasure to be executed by a man of such charm! (*They both bow. The* VICEROY *goes into* PEDRO's *house*) Bolo, have the orchestra stand by.

BOLO

(*To boys offstage*)
Orchestra, stand by. (TRILLO *comes in.*)

TRILLO

(*On the verge of tears*)
Oh, Captain!

SERAFIN

Well, Trillo, this will be a unique performance. Estramudo's last appearance. We ought to double the prices. Announce it, Trillo. Double prices!

TRILLO

(*Drying a tear*)
You are doubtless the most avaricious corpse I have ever wept to see. What good's money once you is gone?

THE PIRATE

SERAFIN

I have no inferiority complex, Trillo, but I am under no illusion that my death will depress the currency. It should, but it won't. Bolo, call beginners. Tell the boys to play up.

BOLO
(*Obeying*)

Beginners—play up, boys. (LIZARDA *comes in.*)

LIZARDA
(*Very flurried*)

If you please, sir, the Governor says you better start. (TRILLO *goes toward her as she exits;* SERAFIN *intervenes.*)

SERAFIN

No, Trillo, no. Do not let your personal life interfere with your art! (*Puts his arms around* TRILLO *and* BOLO) I may be snatched away during the performance. If you don't see me again keep up the tradition of the troupe. (*The two begin to weep*) I bequeath to you the props and my professional secrets. Guard them! Guard them! Trillo, you may have my costumes and my earrings. Bolo, you may have the rabbit— but no matter how hard pressed, don't eat it. Courage! Think of it! Tonight there will be a crowd. For the first time in our history—for the first time, do you realize it, we will be outnumbered by the audience. What a sensation! Overture! (SERAFIN *exits through the curtains of the show tent. Fanfare and music. People, white and colored, but mainly colored,*

179

THE PIRATE

*dressed in their fantastic, gala best, begin to drift in. Offstage
we hear* ESTABAN's *spiel to the incoming audience.*)

ESTABAN

The only chance, Ladies and Gentlemen, the only chance
to see him in person—to see him in the flesh. He makes the
ladies dream and their husbands tremble. Mesmer's favorite
pupil. Reads the past, the present and the future. Foretold
the Battle of Waterloo and the Hundred Days. Foretold all
the childbirths of the Empress of Austria. He knows in advance—he knows in advance. Get in line. Don't crowd—get
in line. (*The* VICEROY's *two lieutenants come in and stroll
over to* ISABELLA's *house as* ISABELLA *comes out. The lieutenants kiss her hand and chat with her.* INES, *the* VICEROY *and*
CAPUCHO *come out of* MANUELA's *house.* LIZARDA *comes out.*
TRILLO *moves toward her, watches her.*)

ISABELLA

(*Looking across—to the* LIEUTENANTS)
That's the Viceroy, isn't it? I've been dying to meet him.
Could you manage an introduction?

INES

(*As she shows the* VICEROY *his chair*)
Shall we sit here, Excellency? Everybody can see us from
here. High visibility. (*She giggles. The* VICEROY *smiles. One
of the* LIEUTENANTS *crosses to the* VICEROY, *whispers in his ear.
The* VICEROY *rises, bows to* INES *and follows the* LIEUTENANT
across the stage to ISABELLA.)

FIRST LIEUTENANT

(*Introducing* VICEROY *to* ISABELLA)

May I have the honor, Excellency, to present Donna Galvez? (*The* VICEROY *bows.*)

ISABELLA

Greetings. You so seldom visit our village.

VICEROY

That is my loss, Señora Galvez.

ISABELLA

I come often to the Capitol and gaze at Government House from outside.

VICEROY

Ah, we shall soon remedy that.

ISABELLA

(*In ecstasy*)

Oh, Excellency! (INES *rises, goes over and takes possession of the* VICEROY, *dragging him away.*)

INES

(*Firmly to* VICEROY)

Don't carry democracy too far, Excellency, stay with me.

ISABELLA

(*Bridling*)

Some people think they're better than anybody else.

THE PIRATE

INES

Some people are right!

VICEROY

(*To* ISABELLA, *soothing her*)

Au revoir, Señora Galvez. (*He bows and starts back across the stage with* INES. MANUELA *comes in and stands in the "box" surveying the scene.*)

INES

(*To* VICEROY)

Did you know that I was once engaged to a Duc? His family objected. The Duc was broken-hearted and so was I —for two weeks.

ISABELLA

(*To the* LIEUTENANTS, *bitterly, staring at* INES)

She thinks she owns the earth. Her husband is a gambler. Mine was an alderman! (*As* INES *and the* VICEROY *turn to go into the box they see* MANUELA.)

INES

Excellency, doesn't my daughter look like me? Same coloring, don't you think? Oh, isn't it gala! In Madrid I always went to first nights with the Marquis de Verdugo.

ESTABAN

(*Enters, selling cocoanuts and sugar cane. He circulates through the crowd.*)

Cocoanuts—full of cool milk—soothes the anxious—cools

182

the passionate. . . . (*One of the troupe comes out and starts his dance. There is applause when he finishes his number.* BOLO *comes on and sings a familiar song. The crowd joins in the song. During this number two white girls come in with a colored attendant. As they pass the* VICEROY'S *box, they bow to him and hurriedly find places to sit. The stage is quite full by this time.*)

INES

Why can't people come in on time? (SERAFIN *comes in in full costume, green mantle, stitched with the signs of the Zodiac and a wonderful tufted hat. A murmur through the crowd.*)

FIRST GIRL

Are you scared?

SECOND GIRL

I am thrilled and scared too.

INES

(*To the girls*)

Sh! (SERAFIN *starts his routine at once; takes off his gloves and rolls them into a bouquet which he hands to* MANUELA. *Then he makes an omelette in a dish and this omelette turns into a rabbit. When the applause for this transformation has died down, he walks down the runway and addresses the crowd. He is in easy rapport with his audience, friendly, humorous, a bit cynical—talking to it in affectionate camaraderie. He is in a pleasant glow, conscious that things have been going pretty well and that the audience is as well disposed toward him as he is to it—in short he indulges in that "comedy of insult" of which perhaps he,* SERAFIN, *was the first practitioner.*)

SERAFIN

(*To the audience*)

And now, Ladies and Gentlemen, honored guest— (*He bows to the* VICEROY, *who returns the bow*) in behalf of my little troupe, these genial virtuosi of the hi-de-ho, may I thank you for your indulgence and appreciation? I am particularly happy that you are pleased this evening, as this is apt to be my farewell performance. Not that this is my first farewell performance—I am old enough to have given many —but this time I think I can rely on our honored guest to make it a genuine farewell. (*He bows ironically to the* VICEROY. *The* VICEROY *bows back.* MANUELA *hangs her head.* PEDRO *glows with pleasure*) Forgive me for bringing in the personal note—but for me as well as for you this is a special occasion. Usually at this time I perform a rope trick—but under the circumstances I thought it might be in questionable taste. . . . I did not want to allow a macabre note to enter the proceedings. After all, we are here to entertain you, not to depress you, and so I skip the rope. (*Laughter from the crowd*) Although let me assure you I manipulate this fluid instrument with a dexterity and ingenuity that has beguiled potentates and plebeians the world over. Therefore I come quickly to the more serious side of our entertainment— an experiment in the new and sensational science of animal magnetism—taught me by its proponent—taught me by the great Mesmer himself. You know, of course, the principles enunciated by the great Mesmer. You know how he divined the influence exerted by the stars on human beings. How he traced this force first to electricity, and then to magnetism. He began his experiment by stroking diseased bodies with magnets and then discarded the magnets when he became conscious of this healing power within himself. This force, Ladies and Gentlemen, flows through us all—in some the current is stronger than in others. When these forces converge, two human beings become as one, the stronger manipulating force drawing out the secrets of the other. Ladies and Gentlemen, there is a new-fangled word to describe this state: Hypnosis! Hypnosis—hypnosis—and the power to induce it was taught me by the great Mesmer himself. And now, Ladies and Gentlemen, before your very eyes I shall perform this experiment! (*At this point, a Gothic curtain comes down with a thud behind* SERAFIN; *it reveals a church spire in a ghostly moonlight. A hush falls on the crowd*) But in order to do so, I shall need the help of one of you. . . . (*Pause—* SERAFIN *looks around*) When I began these experiments, I called for volunteers. This was not always entirely successful. Control cannot be exercised over everyone. I have failed with the recalcitrant, with the confused, with the rebellious, with the evil, with those whose souls are stumpy with greed and envy—in short, Ladies and Gentlemen, to perform this experiment ideally, I need a pure person. Are there any pure people here tonight? (*He smiles*) It's a lot to ask, I know. Purity is very rare. Very rare. Let me see. . . . (*He looks at the* VICEROY) Our distinguished guest? Well, it's too much to expect purity of a politician—he would be the last to claim it. (*The* VICEROY *smiles. He is enjoying himself hugely.* SERA-FIN *keeps looking around.* ISABELLA *lifts her hand eagerly*) Seldom found among the sophisticated . . . (INES *winks at him*) I'm afraid not. Hardly—no—venerable, but not pure . . . (*He continues the search*) It is almost too much to expect. Ah! Ladies and Gentlemen, if we were only all of us back in Arcadia, how easy to perform this experiment! Easy, perhaps, but not interesting. One pure person—fortunately I, the manipulator, do not have to be pure. Fortunately, I . . . (*As he sees* PEDRO) Now, if only, instead of innocence, I were seeking corruption, how easy my task would be. . . . (*His eyes meet* MANUELA'S. *He holds them. There is a pause. Finally, in a whisper, these words escape from* SERAFIN) Nymph, in thy orisons, be all my sins remembered. Purity at last—purity! (*From the moment his eyes rest on* MANUELA'S *the chain of their glance is never broken until the "experiment" is finally over. He walks slowly, holding her with his eyes, across the stage toward her box*) Gracious lady—that you should be here, at my farewell, makes it a blessing indeed. Gracious lady— (*By this time he is very near her. He reaches out his hand to her*) Come—come— As I, Serafin, ask it—my last request—my last request . . . Come—come . . . (MANUELA *rises, already half in a trance. We do not know exactly whether it is a genuine hypnosis or from her desire to obey the man she loves, his dying request. She rises slowly and reaches out her hand to him.* PEDRO *tries to intervene.*)

PEDRO

Manuela—what are you doing?

SERAFIN

(*Pays no attention to* PEDRO, *keeps his eyes on* MANUELA)

Come—you know whatever I ask of you—whatever power I have is for you—is for your happiness—for your soul's salvation and mine. Gracious lady—come. (*By this time,* MANUELA *has risen and, with* SERAFIN's *help, made the low step to the platform.* BOLO *and* TRILLO *bring out stools and place them for* SERAFIN *and* MANUELA *to sit on.*)

PEDRO

(*Protesting violently*)

I forbid this! This is a disgrace, Viceroy. She is my wife!

VICEROY

(*Very much interested*)

This is not a divorce, Pedro. It is an experiment.

SERAFIN

(*Very softly, holding* MANUELA *by his eyes*)

Sit, gracious lady . . . pure spirit, rest. (MANUELA *sits,* SERAFIN *stands before her. He passes his hands over her face.*)

PEDRO

(*Shrieks*)

My wife!

SERAFIN

(*Taking revolving mirror from* TRILLO *and holding it in front of* MANUELA's *eyes*)

Will you please explain to him, Excellency, that this is not passion, it is science.

VICEROY

(*Complying, to* PEDRO)

It's science.

PEDRO

Whatever you call it, I don't like it.

VICEROY

You must be more public-spirited.

INES

He should do that to me. I have so much more to tell!

SERAFIN

(*More softly, to* MANUELA)

Are you afraid of me?

MANUELA

No, no.

SERAFIN

(*Softly*)

I only want what is best for you—you know that.

MANUELA

Yes, I know that.

SERAFIN

Manuela, if you have in your soul any secret conflict, speak freely to me who am your friend. I have only one wish, Manuela, only one . . .

MANUELA

I, too, have only one wish.

SERAFIN

And what is that, Manuela?

MANUELA

I wish, I wish . . .

PEDRO

Black magic! I won't have him practice black magic on my wife!

VICEROY

Please, Pedro . . .

PEDRO

It's an outrage!

ISABELLA

Don't let him stop, Excellency. Maybe she'll tell something vital.

VICEROY

(*To* PEDRO)

This promises to be an amusing experiment. I will not have it spoiled by your bourgeois possessiveness. (*To* SERAFIN) Proceed, Mesmer, with your mesmerism. (*During these interruptions* SERAFIN *and* MANUELA *have not moved an inch, nor have their eyes wavered an instant from each other.*)

SERAFIN

Your wish, Manuela—your wish . . .

189

MANUELA
(*Vaguely*)

I've forgotten. . . .

SERAFIN
(*Patiently*)

Don't worry—there is plenty of time—it will come back to you.

MANUELA

No woman was ever in such a dilemma. . . .

PEDRO
(*Blustering*)

She's in no dilemma, she's very happy.

VICEROY

Please, Pedro.

SERAFIN

You speak of a dilemma, Manuela—what is it?

MANUELA

No woman was ever in such a dilemma.

SERAFIN

That is a large statement, Manuela. In most women's lives dilemmas are frequent.

INES

That was my life. One dilemma after the other.

190

THE PIRATE

SERAFIN

What is your dilemma, Manuela?

MANUELA

It's really laughable.

SERAFIN

I shan't laugh.

MANUELA

My dilemma is that I have found him of whom I dream and he is no better than my husband. In fact, he is . . .

SERAFIN

(*Interrupting*)

Who?

MANUELA

No better.

SERAFIN

This is a bit obscure, Manuela. I don't understand you. What do you mean?

MANUELA

He is so romantic and reckless—in fact, he is quite adolescent. I don't know what to do with him.

SERAFIN

Has he made no suggestions?

MANUELA

Oh, yes, but none that I can accept. You see, I am a wife.

191

SERAFIN

It seems to me we've heard that somewhere before.

MANUELA

Men can wander about with stars in their eyes, but women —especially when they are in love . . .

SERAFIN

Yes?

MANUELA

Women have to think about the future. You see, I am not a Bohemian.

SERAFIN

Pure soul, pure soul . . .

MANUELA

Romance is all very well for escape, but when you meet a real person whom you could love you don't need romance, and you're irritated by recklessness. You want the real man— to have him and to hold him—you want to take no chances with him. I want him legitimately, if possible, illegitimately if not possible.

SERAFIN

(*Murmurs*)

Pure soul.

MANUELA

I am not a pure soul. I am an unhappy, love-starved woman. You can't be pure when you're frustrated.

INES
(*With a giggle*)
It's even hard when you're not frustrated.

PEDRO
(*He can resist no longer*)
Excellency, how much longer are you going to permit this?

VICEROY
Indefinitely.

SERAFIN
Go on, Manuela.

MANUELA
If I had the man I love, then I could be pure. I could be pure in my devotion to him. Purity then would be a joy.

INES
There speaks my daughter.

ISABELLA
She's a hussy. (MANUELA *laughs a little*.)

SERAFIN
Why do you laugh?

MANUELA
I was rather wicked, I must say.

THE PIRATE

SERAFIN

Pure soul, can you be wicked?

MANUELA

Don't call me pure soul—it irritates me. I was wicked.

SERAFIN

How?

MANUELA

I tortured him.

SERAFIN

Whom?

MANUELA

My husband.

SERAFIN

How?

MANUELA

By telling him I had a lover.

SERAFIN

And you have no lover?

MANUELA

Not yet.

SERAFIN

Pure soul.

ISABELLA

She's hovering on the brink.

194

THE PIRATE

VICEROY

(Drily, to PEDRO)

Congratulations!

SERAFIN

Manuela, was this a device merely?

MANUELA

Yes. I wanted to annoy him.

SERAFIN

Did you succeed?

MANUELA

Oh, wonderfully. I thought he would burst. In fact, he did.

SERAFIN

(With a gesture toward PEDRO)

At the moment, he seems restive—but intact.

MANUELA

In his desire to hurt me he lost all control of himself—and nearly burst out with the truth.

SERAFIN

And what was that, Manuela?

MANUELA

The Sultan with all those wives of his . . .

SERAFIN

Well?

MANUELA

He was henpecked! (PEDRO *gets up, protesting violently.*)

PEDRO

Excellency, this is immoral. I won't listen.

SERAFIN

I am only trying to get at the truth, Excellency.

PEDRO

The truth is immoral. It shouldn't be spoken in public.

VICEROY

Don't you want to hear about the Sultan? I am longing to hear about the Sultan.

PEDRO
(Shouts)

Fairy tales!

VICEROY

Fairy tales are a form of truth also, Pedro.

PEDRO

I'm ill. I've got an attack coming on.

INES

Go in and lie down in your hammock, darling.

196

THE PIRATE

I think I will.

Sweet dreams. (PEDRO *goes into his house.* SERAFIN *motions* TRILLO *and* BOLO *to follow him. They go out after* PEDRO.)

(Settling himself comfortably, to SERAFIN)
Now we can go comfortably into the domestic difficulties of the Sultan.

Manuela, what has the Sultan to do with you and your husband?

Don't you see? My husband disposed of them.

Disposed of whom?

The Sultan's nine wives. He got rid of them. Took them off and drowned them like so many kittens. He got paid by the head. Just like Pedro. If someone offered him enough, he'd drown me.

Manuela, you say your husband did that—your husband— are you sure?

MANUELA

Oh, yes, Estramudo, I am sure. Why do I call you Estramudo?

SERAFIN

Why not, Manuela?

MANUELA

Because you are not.

SERAFIN

How do you know?

MANUELA

Because you only said you were to interest me. (*Sensation among the audience. The* VICEROY *leans forward.* MANUELA *rather begins to prattle*) You didn't have to—you interested me anyway.

SERAFIN

Really—in what way?

MANUELA

I don't know—I think it was just the way you circled round me. Everywhere I went, there I came smack up against you. I'd never been circled like that before.

VICEROY

(*To* SERAFIN)

Can you keep her on the subject, Mesmer?

198

SERAFIN

(*To* VICEROY)

I'll try. (*To* MANUELA) You say I told you I was Estramudo to interest you. And did it interest you?

MANUELA

Oh, yes, very much.

SERAFIN

Why?

MANUELA

Because of all men alive, Estramudo seemed the farthest removed from my husband.

SERAFIN

You wanted to get away from your husband?

MANUELA

Oh, yes—oh, yes.

INES

Who doesn't?

SERAFIN

Why did you want to get away from your husband?

MANUELA

Because my husband isn't interested in me. If he is, he never shows it.

SERAFIN

And this causes you unhappiness?

MANUELA

It bores me. My life is empty. That is why I dreamt of Estramudo. But now I have no one to dream of.

SERAFIN

Is Estramudo exhausted?

MANUELA

That's what's so sad. You see—Estramudo is my husband. (*Sensation—the* VICEROY *leans forward. Crowd gasps.*)

SERAFIN

Manuela, this is rather startling. You say that your husband, the estimable Pedro . . .

MANUELA

Oh, he's a terrible fraud.

SERAFIN

In what way?

MANUELA

He's reformed. It's awful to live with a reformed character. They make you pay for their early transgressions. They double-discipline you to give themselves an illusion of virtue.

200

THE PIRATE

INES

I didn't know my daughter was so penetrating.

SERAFIN

(*Gently*)

But when did you discover that your husband was really Estramudo?

MANUELA

Just a few hours ago.

SERAFIN

But you already know one false Estramudo. Isn't it possible that your husband is another?

MANUELA

No, it is not possible.

SERAFIN

How do you know?

MANUELA

Because it's been proved to me.

SERAFIN

How?

MANUELA

It's been proved that he's the genuine Estramudo.

INES

That lump!

THE PIRATE

ISABELLA

That bluenose! I'll never believe it.

SERAFIN

Manuela, this may be an invention of your husband. How do you know it is the truth?

MANUELA

Because I've seen the jeweled medallion the Sultan gave him out of gratitude. It's inscribed, "To Estramudo." It says, "For taking a load off my mind—from his friend the Sultan."

SERAFIN

Manuela, where is this jewel?

MANUELA

He carries it in a little bag around his neck.

INES

I always wondered what was in that little bag. He'd never let me touch it. (*On this disclosure the* VICEROY *has risen and gone into the house, following* PEDRO.)

SERAFIN

Go on, Manuela.

MANUELA

And under the floor of our barn I found the most fabulous jewels! Imagine—wouldn't you have thought that just once he'd have had the generous impulse to say, "Manuela, just for tonight, put on Catherine's stomacher"? But he never did —he never let me have the stomacher. You have no idea the difference in a woman's psychology a few trinkets makes. . . . Why, he never even gave me so much as an earring . . . !

SERAFIN

Awake, Manuela—return to yourself—think of nothing—Manuela, awake.

MANUELA

(*Prattling on*)

Not one earring . . . ! I could never marry a man who wandered in and out of ladies' bedrooms on cobwebs. I'd have insomnia.

SERAFIN

I wish I could give you insomnia right now.

MANUELA

Even his childishness was adorable. If he were my husband —ah!—then dream would not have to go beyond reality. The near hill as wonder-making as the far hill—the rose outside the window, the fragrance of the invisible, ideal rose—the imagined caress merging with the actual—my husband and my lover both—that would be—that would be . . .

SERAFIN

It would be heaven, Manuela! But wake—I beg you—wake . . . (*The crowd begins to surge nearer.*)

INES

What's the matter? Can't you wake her?

ISABELLA

What's the matter? What's gone wrong?

SERAFIN

(*Holding off the crowd with a gesture*)

Don't come near her—don't touch her, she may die. (*Awed, the crowd desists. The* VICEROY *comes out of the house, the two soldiers following with the pinioned* PEDRO.)

INES

What is it, Excellency? Why have you bound my son-in-law?

VICEROY

He is not your son-in-law! He never was your son-in-law!

INES

What?

VICEROY

This isn't Pedro Vargas. Pedro Vargas was the captain of a ship he scuttled. The Captain went down with his ship and he took his name. He is the real Estramudo!

PEDRO

(*Defiant*)

Yes! All these years she's dreamt about me and all the time it was I! (*Sensation from the crowd.*)

SERAFIN
(*Desperate over* MANUELA)

Manuela—awake . . .

VICEROY
(*To his men*)

Take him away! We shall send you to the Capitol at government expense.

PEDRO
(*Pleading*)

Mercy!

VICEROY

Why should I be merciful? You have never shown mercy to others. However, we are engaged in a desperate war with that fiercely marine people, the Berbers. I may give you a captaincy. Your piratical experience should come in handy.

PEDRO

I shall fight for you as only a reformed character can fight!

VICEROY

We may try you. (*Nods to the men who take him off*) Legally, Manuela is now a widow.

SERAFIN
(*Fired by this sudden vista, his voice rising*)

Widow! Manuela—awake—awake to widowhood!

INES

If that doesn't wake her, nothing will!

VICEROY

What's wrong, Mesmer? It seems easier to induce a trance than to get out of it.

MANUELA

(*Still prattling*)

The trouble with me is that I'm a homebody. He was willing to risk his life for me. . . . Imagine, his life . . .

SERAFIN

Awake, Manuela . . . (*He blows a horn and rings a bell in front of her—no effect.*)

SERAFIN

Oh, God, I can't wake her! She won't wake! (*The crowd surges toward him, some threatening. They shout suggestions.*)

LIZARDA

Mistress—beloved mistress—please wake up. It's what they call a catalepsy!

ISABELLA

(*Indignant, to* SERAFIN)

What are you doing to my best friend?

CAPUCHO

I'll have you jailed for this.

BOLO

Use voodoo, get her out of it with voodoo.

TRILLO

Try rattlesnakes' skins and vinegar.

ONE OF THE CROWD

That cured my grandmother.

ANOTHER

Cut her laces.

BOLO

They say lizard's milk and chili . . .

GIRL IN CROWD

Burn a feather under her nose.

LIZARDA

Is she alive or dead?

ANOTHER GIRL

She's dead—she's dead.

ANOTHER GIRL

A priest—send for the priest.

SERAFIN

Sh!

VICEROY

Have you lost your skill, Mesmer? Where is your power?

SERAFIN

Let me try again. Stand back. (*They all stand aside. The singing begins.* SERAFIN *passes his hands over* MANUELA's *face*) Manuela—it is I. It is Serafin—it is my love—it is our future —it is our happiness—it is reality.

MANUELA
(*Sits up suddenly*)

Where am I?

SERAFIN
(*Close to her*)

You are with me, Manuela—you are with me—forever and ever.

MANUELA

Oh, this is a lovely dream.

VICEROY
(*Who has been watching with the others*)

What is there about this town that induces matrimony?

INES

The Gulf Stream.

SERAFIN
(*Picking* MANUELA *up in his arms*)

I lied to you, my dearest. Do you forgive me?

MANUELA

There are two kinds of lies—lies like Pedro's, intended to

pervert the truth—and lies like yours, which widen the borders of experience, and open the windows of the imagination. They may some day blossom into those flowers of the soul that are called ideals. I shall follow you—I shall follow you to the end. (SERAFIN *starts walking toward* MANUELA'S *house, carrying* MANUELA *in his arms. The crowd lifts its voice in song, a joyous epithalamium.*)

Curtain

9160
79a